24x 9/00 ✓ 10/00
29x10/05 ✓ 12/05

11/48 (21) ✓ 6/49

HOW TO
READ AND PROFIT
FROM
FINANCIAL NEWS

Also by Gerald Krefetz

HOW TO

READ

AND

PROFIT

FROM

FINANCIAL

NEWS

SECOND EDITION

GERALD KREFETZ

Dearborn
Financial Publishing, Inc.

To Dorothy, Nadine, Adriene

This publication is designed to provide accurate and authoritative information in regard to the subject matter covered. It is sold with the understanding that the publisher is not engaged in rendering legal, accounting or other professional service. If legal advice or other expert assistance is required, the services of a competent professional person should be sought.

Editor in Chief: Caroline Carney
Managing Editor: Jack Kiburz
Associate Project Editor: Stephanie C. Schmidt
Interior Design: Lucy Jenkins
Cover Design: Jill Shimabukuro

© 1984 and 1995 by Gerald Krefetz

Published by Dearborn Financial Publishing, Inc.

Printed in the United States of America

95 96 97 10 9 8 7 6 5 4 3 2 1

Library of Congress Cataloging-in-Publication Data
Krefetz, Gerald.
   How to read and profit from financial news/Gerald Krefetz. —
2nd ed.
      p. cm.
   Includes index.
   ISBN 0-7931-1557-4 (cloth)
   1. Investments. 2. Securities. 3. Stock exchanges. 4.Commodity exchanges. 5. Newspapers—Sections, columns, etc.—Finance.
   I. Title. II. Krefetz, Gerald.
   HG4521.K72 1995
   332.6'78—dc20   95-4706
                                                     CIP

CONTENTS

PREFACE

I n the last decade, since an earlier version of this book appeared, the financial world has moved at warp speed. A dizzying array of events has affected the value of your money and the worth of your financial assets: the Louvre currency accord; the 1987 stock market collapse; the Gulf war; change of political administrations in Washington; the unification of Germany; the end of the Soviet Union and the emergence of Russia and the independent republics; ethnic strife in the former Yugoslavia; the rebirth of South Africa; the boom-bust cycle of Japan; the development of new financial instruments such as derivatives. Keeping up with it all is nearly a full-time occupation.

But don't despair. Technology in communications has kept pace with this information explosion. Coverage is now facilitated by radio, television, fax, cellular telephones, personal computers, workstations and mainframes. Information services inundate recipients with texts, graphics and data via radio waves, cables, lasers and fiber optics. Never before has so much fact, forecast and prophecy been available. So much for the good news.

The bad news is: How much of today's financial page or morning business broadcast did you understand? Chances are you found the glut of facts and figures too discouraging to tackle, or, if you did make the effort, you came away wondering just how the price changes and emerging trends will affect your own life and finances. In the last decade, the "language" of money has changed dramatically. New words have been coined and old concepts have taken on new meanings. It is now imperative for everyone who earns a salary to understand the basics of finance if they are to stay abreast of the wealth of financial and economic news with which they are confronted every day. Most of the information you need to be a successful do-it-yourself investor is public knowledge. It is easily found in the press and news broadcasts, or it can be sought in the electronic world through personal computers and word processors. Financial and business news is the bloodstream of the free enterprise system, heralding opportunities, warning of pitfalls. There are, however, two major problems facing investors and potential investors. First, in this age of exploding information, how does one separate the useful from the useless, the information that is nice to know from that which you need to know? The abundance of news can be overwhelming, and a glut of information is almost as bad as not having any.

Second, how do you know wnat the news really means? Is there some special key that gives money managers and insiders greater insight into generally accessible facts and figures? Do you need a master's degree in business administration to make sense of the financial news? The dangers of missed information, misinformation and misunderstood information are enormous—foregone opportunities, reduced savings, low rates of return, lost capital. And learning what you don't know with your own hard-earned dollars can be an expensive education. Studies and polls reveal that most people do not fully comprehend the meaning of some very basic financial data. Consequently, they make financial decisions in response to the news, but without really understanding what that news means in terms of the mechanics of the market. This book attempts to clarify and reveal the meaning of financial information and to explain the different markets and how the news affects them.

Although inside information and expensive private studies by analysts and economists (who tend to be wrong as often as they are right) can occasionally be valuable, they can't possibly be completely up to date; there is an inevitable time lapse between the news report and the publication of the expert's analysis. It is the public distribution and proper understanding of the news that makes for judicious and profitable investments. Of course, this is no easy matter in today's complex business environment. Never before has the public been offered such a bewildering variety of investment vehicles.

This book offers no magic formulas for surefire profit. What it does provide is a straightforward, if occasionally opinionated, description of how markets work, and insights into what is generally considered important and relevant information in making investment decisions. Along the way, just about everyone makes some wrong moves, and errors in judgment are always more easily seen in hindsight. Unlike Mark Twain's cat, who sat once upon a hot stove and never again sat on a cold one, investors can learn from being burnt. The better informed you are, the less chance there is that your lessons will be painful or unexpected. Through a systematic, rational understanding of markets, it is possible to improve performance and achieve the sense that you control your investment destiny. To assist you, this book offers a quick tour of the nuts and bolts as well as the dynamics of the capitalist workshop.

CHAPTER 1

Why a Stock Market

*It takes three generations or one good guess in the stock
market to make a gentleman.*

—Anonymous

The securities markets of America are responsible for
amassing the nation's wealth and putting it to work in
industry, commerce and business. Thanks to their success,
the United States has a six-trillion-dollar gross national product (GNP) and one of the highest standards of living in the
world. Other nations had bourses and exchanges long before
this country was founded, but nowhere has the capital market been so efficient or so powerful in husbanding and har-
nessing the resources of a nation. Today, publicly owned
corporations not only dominate American business but also
constitute a far greater part of the economy than is the case in
other countries.

The main function of the stock exchanges is not to enrich
the financial community or to provide a "crapshoot" for the
idle rich (two often-heard criticisms) but to generate funds to
be employed in private business ventures. When the New
York Stock Exchange (NYSE) was founded in 1792 under a
spreading buttonwood tree in front of 68 Wall Street, it dealt
primarily in the relatively new and untried consolidated
bonds (public stock, as it was then called) of the United States
government.

Since then, thousands of companies have "gone public"; that is, they have issued publicly traded shares that represent a fractional ownership of their enterprises. The stock exchanges, including the over-the-counter market, are the mechanical hearts of the free enterprise system: They facilitate the trading of securities. Trading is the lifeblood and lubricant of the system; it gives the whole financial structure nourishment and the necessary liquidity. Without such liquidity, the complex system would grind to a halt, rather like a hydraulic system without fluid. Liquidity enables both individuals and institutions to cash in their investments—to pay their bills and liabilities or simply to put their money in other investments with greater potential, for nothing remains static in the investment world.

Thus one of the chief characteristics of the American capital market is the ability of traders to enter and exit on little notice. Unlike some investment vehicles (such as farmland, second homes, tax shelter partnerships, antique furniture and assorted collectibles), the highly developed capital market enables any player—investor, speculator, pension fund or foreign country—to play or cash in his or her "marbles" virtually instantaneously. This instant liquidity is one of the market's greatest attractions.

The Capitalists and Their Markets

At last count, a majority of Americans were directly or indirectly involved in the nation's financial markets. The most extensive survey, conducted for the New York Stock Exchange, found 51.4 million individual shareowners in 1990; an additional 200 million individuals owned securities indirectly through retirement plans, insurance policies, savings banks, mutual funds and other instruments. In short, probably three out of four citizens are "capitalists," whether they realize it or not.

A short profile of the American capitalist looks something like this: 63 percent are male and 37 percent female; the median age is 43, the median portfolio close to $11,400 and the median family income about $43,800. California has the highest number of capitalists, North Dakota the lowest. Parenthetically, the greatest density of millionaires is in Idaho, followed by Maine. College graduates own more securities than any other group, while professionals and those in technical occupations are the most likely investors. The typical transaction on the New York Stock Exchange is $12,289, compared with $5,576 on the other exchanges. The average price of an NYSE share is about $35.

In recent years, the individual investor has been eclipsed by institutions—those behemoths with other people's money—which now account for more than 43.6 percent of the market value of all shares on the NYSE. Institutions, more than ever before, tend to dominate the market, especially in companies with large capitalization, where they frequently hold more than 20 percent of the shares. The center of the capital markets is the NYSE, which trades 85 percent of all the stock in the country and is generally regarded as the busiest exchange in the world, measured by dollar volume. Indeed, in 1993 the NYSE had 129 billion shares listed for the 2,904 companies registered on the exchange, and nearly 66 billion shares were traded through its 506 member organizations. The value of membership in the NYSE has fluctuated as much as some of the stock averages. During the 1969 recession, a seat on the exchange sold for a record high of $515,000, an indication that membership does not endow members with prophetic foresight or crystal ball–gazing ability. And in 1977, in the midst of the 1975–79 recovery and expansion, the membership fee fell to $35,000. Since then, prices have recovered; recent seats have exchanged hands for between $800,000 and $900,000. Clearly, the trading of seats on the exchange is not a leading economic indicator. Still, the price of a seat has gone up considerably from the original membership price of $400 nearly two centuries ago.

The other market on Wall Street is the American Stock Exchange (AMEX), previously known as the Curb because of its early outdoor location. Its listing requirements for trading are not as rigorous as those for the NYSE; consequently, the AMEX is frequently thought of as the home of emerging growth companies—companies that have had some public exposure on the over-the-counter market but are not quite ready for the Big Board. In recent years, the AMEX list has been heavily populated with energy companies, and these oil and gas stocks give the AMEX index a volatile character. Moreover, they tend to sell at a price-earnings ratio of about 50 percent more than NYSE companies.

Finally, investors and traders can buy shares in the rapidly expanding over-the-counter (OTC) market, or from the National Association of Security Dealers Automated Quotations (Nasdaq). This market has no central headquarters; rather, it is a network of telephone and computer/fax communications that links thousands of brokerage houses across the country. In the effort to streamline and consolidate operations, the network has been computerized so that brokers can find out through their desktop terminals what the current market price of a stock is and who makes the market. Though computers have revolutionized the OTC market, the nature of trading remains much as it has always been: the buying and selling of shares, like any other commodity.

However, the buying and selling of shares is different from the trading that takes place on the exchanges. Market makers in the Nasdaq market represent themselves. They are dealing from their own accounts with their own inventories of securities; they are principals in the transactions and make their money not on brokerage commissions but on the profit from each trade. The market maker buys wholesale and sells retail, as any merchant does, profiting from the markup (or markdown) of approximately 5 percent—though the figure can vary considerably.

Consequently, the customer or his agent (his broker) is dealing on a net basis. No commissions apply other than what one's broker may charge. Trading on the exchanges, on the other hand, is based on prices set by an auction system. Ideally, buyers and sellers reach an equilibrium in determining price. When there is a disequilibrium—that is, a lack of or too many buyers or sellers at the market price—then specialists in the stock (who have been assigned a number of securities to trade by the exchange and who are responsible for maintaining a fair and orderly market) step in. They then trade from their books of previously placed but as yet unexecuted orders or, if that isn't sufficient, from their own accounts.

In the OTC market, price is determined by the market makers—the 2, 7, sometimes even 18 traders who make a market in a given security. Prices differ from maker to maker, but they tend to hover or bunch in one area. In the daily press, the OTC market price is a representative price. Not all OTC issues are on the National Association of Securities Dealers' computer: Issues that are traded less frequently have prices and market makers published in the "pink sheets," a daily publication of the National Quotation Bureau. The important factor is that OTC prices are negotiated between customer and dealer, whereas prices listed on an exchange are established through an auction process presided over by the specialist, although most of the time prices are still determined by the buyers and sellers.

New public companies are but one kind of security traded in the OTC market. All sorts of issues have found a place here, from corporate giants and financial institutions, such as insurance companies and banks, to foreign shares and government bonds. So, although the OTC market is often thought of as the home of untried companies and risky securities, it should be remembered that it is also the home of old, established corporations, securities of government agencies and multinational companies. The choice is as broad as the risk. In response to prodding from Congress, the Securities and Exchange Commission (SEC) and the investing public, the securities markets have taken some major steps to rationalize their operations and move toward one overall, integrated market. Economic logic dictates that the investors will obtain better prices if there is less fragmentation. In 1971, the National Association of Securities Dealers, Inc. (NASD) set up the first computerized trading system, which tied together broker-dealer firms. Members could call up the quotation system on their own computers and query it for the best bid and asked prices. (The bid is the highest price anyone has offered for a given security; the asked is the price at which shares are offered for sale.) In 1982, the NASD set up a new quote system, the National Market System (NMS), which not only gives prices but also requires its members to enter all transactions into the electronic system so they can be flashed to the thousands of terminals around the world. The companies in the NMS will eventually include the 1,600 most active OTC securities.

Progress has also been made in the exchanges with a consolidated tape that reports trades in all common stock listed on the NYSE and the AMEX as well as regionally listed securities. Moreover, the Intermarket Trading System links all the exchanges and gives an investor the best price through the Composite Quotation System. Finally, in the fourth market, a computerized trading network among institutions, Instinet, completely bypasses intermediaries and exchanges. Whether or not all these different markets will lend themselves to total unification is doubtful, but the investor is certainly better served by the freer competition of integrated markets.

Before examining how the markets work, it is useful to look at the financial structure of the companies whose stocks are publicly traded. Every year, in the spirit of American entrepreneurialism, a vast number of new businesses are created. And every year, the figure increases substantially. Unfortunately, most will wither on the vine. Within two years, probably half will have ceased to exist, and at the end of five years, 80 percent or 85 percent will be only memories. This high fatality rate for new business ventures is the price we pay for an open, competitive economy. The reasons for failure range from undercapitalization (too little start-up money) to overimagination (too many pipe dreams), in addition to a whole assortment of management problems that can turn from critical to terminal in short order. Nevertheless, there are 15 million business entities in the United States. Though most of them are privately owned, there are 40,000 publicly owned companies and about 6,000 whose shares are actively and openly traded on the securities exchanges and in the OTC market.

In addition, several thousand foreign companies are also available to the American investor. Finally, every year hundreds of companies take the plunge and "go public." Almost all these public companies are legal corporations rather than proprietorships or partnerships. The following story is typical of the hundreds of companies that reach a critical point in their growth. Under the austere laws of economics, most businesses must expand or die. Naturally, the founder of the company in the following example chooses to grow.

Capitalizing the Widget Works

When the inventor of the new left-handed widget decides to share his product with the world, he founds the Widget Works. As two out of three entrepreneurs do, he uses his own and his family's funds to get started. Before long, it's obvious that he will need more money. When the local bank turns him down (he has no track record and no collateral), he approaches his friends and acquaintances. The Widget Works is about to end its life as a sole proprietorship and become a corporation.

A corporation serves the interest of the founder for a number of reasons. For one thing, it has a life of its own, separate and distinct from its founder's. Therefore it can endure indefinitely, although it can also be liquidated at any time at the option of the owners. Also, ownership interest in the corporation is transferable. A corporation has legal status in raising funds. And last but not least, one of the main reasons corporations were devised, at the start of the 16th century, was that they limit the personal liability of the founder to his (or her, in another example) original contribution. Regardless of debts and the subsequent bankruptcy of the corporation, the shareowners (or shareholders) will never be assessed for additional monies. (If you decide to invest directly in foreign markets, rather than through foreign shares, which are represented in the United States by American depositary receipts [ADR], you should be aware that some foreign issues go public on a partially paid basis. You will be called upon, at some future time, to come up with a final payment.) Thus, shareowners' personal fortunes are safe from judgments, creditors, wars, depressions, acts of nature and any other fate that may befall a business.

To be sure, there are some drawbacks to incorporating. Corporations are costly to form; they are subject to greater regulation; they are limited to activities spelled out in their charters; and their earnings are subject to double taxation, once at the corporate level and again when those earnings are distributed as dividends to shareholders. Despite these added complexities, the Widget Works is incorporated, and one of its first acts is to raise money by selling shares in the enterprise.

A company's capitalization, or capital structure, is especially significant since it can determine the size, growth rate, financial standing and a series of other critical aspects of its future. In most beginning or relatively new ventures, the founder (and his partners) own 100 percent of the company. In raising new funds, the founder, known also in legal terms as the parent, sells a portion of his equity, or ownership interest, in the new corporation. The ratio of what he sells to what he keeps, the amount of money he wishes to raise, and the control he wishes to maintain are all subject to negotiation between the founder and the potential group of investors. For established companies, this fundraising function is undertaken by an investment banking firm. However, a new company rarely has the product or the profitability to interest an investment banking firm. The most the founder of the Widget Works can hope for is to interest a venture capitalist— an individual or investment group such as a government-registered but private Small Business Investment Company (SBIC)—to take a position in the company's stock.

At this point in raising capital, the new corporation runs into the federal securities laws. Since printing stock certificates is not dissimilar from printing money, it is no surprise that the government is concerned with the issuance of shares. The basic securities laws—the Securities Act of 1933 and the Securities Exchange Act of 1934—are the by-product of the Great Depression and the boom-and-bust era of the 1920s. They attempt to regulate the marketplace, to remove some of the abuses of a free market and to protect the investor from the unscrupulous. Part of their success rests on the principle of full disclosure, the democratic notion that if the investor is fully informed he or she will act wisely. Therefore, it is the responsibility of the companies engaged in raising money from the public to reveal all relevant material concerning the founder, the corporation, the product, the competition, the market and so on. If the company is attempting to raise more than $1.5 million from the public at large, it must register a notification with the SEC, the federal agency that polices the securities laws. If the Widget Works had found 35 or fewer people to fund it, it could have had a private placement of its shares, and no SEC registration would have been necessary. Unable to go this route, the founder of the Widget Works decides to sell 100,000 shares at $10 per share out of a total issued capitalization of 250,000 shares, thus leaving him with three-fifths, or 60 percent, of the company. He retains majority control while the corporation receives the proceeds of the sale—$1,000,000 less expenses.

The Widget Works has decided to use equity financing: By offering stock, the founder is sharing ownership with the investing public. But remember, shareholder democracy is, in the last analysis, a plutocracy. It is the shares that have the votes, not the holders of the shares, and the majority of the shares remain in the founder's possession. In the past some companies, such as The New York Times Company, have further attempted to curtail shareholder democracy by issuing classes of common stock—class A, class B. Different rights belong to different classes. Though there are many variations, the most common and important difference is whether the shares have voting privileges in the business of the corporation, such as voting for directors, accountants, mergers and acquisitions. Increasingly, corporations issue one kind of common stock, but there are exceptions, and certainly there are still different classes in the marketplace.

Before issuing public shares, a company must provide each potential investor with an investment memorandum known as a prospectus. This fulfills the company's obligation to the SEC for full disclosure. A prospectus is chock-full of information, but perhaps the most pertinent data have to do with dilution. The investors in the Widget Works purchased shares for $10 apiece. Setting aside the underlying value (which will be discussed later), the investors' shares are immediately devalued, since the $1 million reflects the worth not of the 100,000 shares that were purchased, but of the total issued capitalization of 250,000. And these 250,000 shares are now worth $4 apiece. To look at it another way, the new shareholders are paying off or rewarding the founder for his time, energy, and imagination in creating the enterprise. His stock now takes on real, tangible value with this first underwriting of the company's shares. It is his payday for all the years of dreaming, planning and striving to build a company.

The founder could have financed his company another way. He could have relied on some form of debt. Obviously, the reason many founders and new companies turn to the equities market is simply because they have run out of money and have borrowed all the funds they can.

To Borrow or Not To Borrow?

Investors should be aware of the kinds of borrowing a company may undertake and the consequences for its capital structure. Depending on how the business conducts its finances, the investor may decide to lend money—that is, purchase corporate bonds—rather than purchase ownership through shares. Some new companies are in the happy position of being able to borrow, and, of course, companies with any business history can "bank" their experience. They are able to obtain lines of credit from commercial banks; they may borrow against their inventory, plant and equipment; they may sell their accounts receivables to a factor or money-lender. These are all relatively expensive, short-term arrangements, the expedients of financing day-to-day or season-to-season trade.

Long-term debt, on the other hand, serves another purpose. It enables one to build a business, to enhance the overall value of the enterprise by investing borrowed funds in buildings, factories, machinery or whatever other equipment the firm needs in order to operate and grow. A lender or creditor has the first or prior claim to the income of the business to service his debt and the first claim on funds when his debt matures. This first claim simply means that creditors get paid before the equity or share owners.

There are some disadvantages to borrowing money, especially in an inflationary period. Although it may appear that debtors are better served by inflation than creditors because they are able to pay back in cheaper dollars, that assumption has a couple of flaws: (1) inflationary periods do not last forever and are invariably followed by periods of disinflation and deflation, and (2) a double-digit interest rate obligation becomes increasingly onerous when current rates fall to single-digit levels. Other disadvantages of long-term borrowing, regardless of interest rates or the state of the economy, are as follows:

- If a company borrows now, it may not be able to borrow later. Some business executives (though they are definitely a minority) think that borrowing should be a last resort.
- Debt service—that is, interest payments—is a fixed charge that can distort the corporation's true earnings picture. Such long-term borrowing is called "trading on the equity of the corporation." Borrowing adds leverage to company earnings, which accents the losses and gains.
- The greater the fixed charges against earnings, the less the financial flexibility that remains with company management. Debt obligations preempt use of the cash flow.
- Heavy debt service can throw the company into insolvency and/or bankruptcy in a period of reduced earnings.

There are, naturally, some advantages to long-term borrowing if properly managed:

- Trading on the equity has a positive side to it if the company can earn more on the borrowed funds than it must pay out in interest. Most borrowers assume that their return on the funds will exceed their costs.
- Some major sources of institutional funds prefer, or are legally obliged, to lend money rather than buy equity.

This provides access to funds for unseasoned but profitable corporations.
- Borrowing money does not dilute the owners' equity. If the company is extraordinarily successful, only the stockholders share in that success.

A company is fortunate if it has the option of considering debt as an alternative to equity financing. Long-term debt is usually represented by issuing bonds that will mature in 10, 20 or 30 years. Consequently, anyone underwriting a bond issue must have some confidence that the company will be around for quite awhile

The Annual Report: What It Is and How To Read It

Every company, publicly owned or not, has developed a history—good, bad or indifferent. This history is important to potential investors, for it is the track record of corporate accomplishments and the measuring stick of financial virtue. It is particularly important for companies undertaking the first public offering of their shares.

A business's accomplishments are revealed in two ways: through what the company says about itself and what others say about it—the official and unofficial views of what the business has done and perhaps will do. The official, or corporate, version of a company's history is summed up yearly in its annual report. This publication is required by the SEC for all businesses with registered securities, and it must be issued within ninety days after the close of the fiscal year. Some banks and insurance companies are exempt from the SEC but must file with state and local authorities.

The annual report in its official guise, as filed with the SEC, is known as Form 10K—a bare-bones, no-frills, typed document that has none of the sex appeal of the glossy brochures published by many companies. Apart from the photographs and graphics, the information is identical, though abbreviated in its promotional form. The slick edition is sent to shareholders, but anyone can receive Form

10K, free of charge, from the company. Included in the annual report are all the key data with which to evaluate a company, including:

- Total sales
- Sales and pre-tax operating income
- Balance sheet
- Income statement
- Surplus or retained earnings
- The source and application of funds
- The number of shares under option
- An auditor's statement
- The roster of directors and company executives

Presented in columns, the data are given for the last three or five years to allow easy comparison.

The annual report is a company's public face, especially if its product does not come into direct contact with the customer. Naturally, the company attempts to look good, to place its best foot forward, particularly in the glossy edition, within the dictates of full disclosure. From the president's letter to the final footnotes, the presentation is geared to enhance the corporate image. For this reason, some professional market analysts are extremely critical of annual reports in general, claiming that they are too self-serving and not worth reading.

No doubt there is some truth to that assertion; but if the reader keeps that bias in mind, these reports can serve as an important primary source of information—especially for companies that do not have a large following of researchers, brokers, analysts and financial publications. The report gives the investor a quick tour of the company, what its major divisions are doing and what they are gearing up to accomplish in the next year. Since it is as close as most investors will ever get to the physical plant, factory or office, the report is a window on the operations.

Of course, it is the statistical data that form a veritable scorecard of the company. Most of the selected financial data are straightforward, lending themselves to immediate comparison. Benjamin Graham, the dean of security analysis, once remarked that even in a world of sophisticated econometric models devised by academic and professional economists, all a successful investor needed to know was some basic arithmetic. That still holds true.

There are several standard features in every annual report. First, there is the letter from the chairperson or president of the company, which paints a general picture of corporate progress and anticipates the business climate for the coming year. Next is an overview or summary of specific operations, new products, acquisitions or divestitures, and management changes. As might be expected, the information tends to be upbeat and positive, brimming with confidence.

What follows is usually a discussion of the financial operations and resulting condition of the firm. For example, the effect of change in inventory valuation, the consequences of inflation, the effects of a major disaster such as a fire or flood, the potential of a new line of business—all will receive close attention in management's discussion of the company's financial condition.

Then come the basic documents of every annual report: the balance sheet, the income statement, the changes in stockholders' equity and the statement of changes in financial position. These four tables are usually followed by notes to the financial statements, footnotes referred to earlier and now spelled out in detail. Finally, the accuracy of the report is attested to by the company's independent auditors. Reports may conclude with additional matter on the company's markets, historical stock prices, dividends, and the roster of directors and corporate executives.

The balance sheet is a summary of the overall value of the company on a given date. The picture it offers has been frozen in time, rather like a snapshot of a waterfall. First it lists all the assets:

- *Current assets:* cash in the till; accounts receivable (accounts not yet received); value of inventory—finished product, work in progress and raw materials
- *Fixed (or long-term) assets:* property or real estate, plant, equipment (less depreciation allowances)
- *Other assets:* intangibles (licenses, good will)

The sum of these items appears on the balance sheet as the "Total Assets." These are followed by liabilities and stockholders' equity, as follows:

- *Current liabilities:* notes due within one year, accounts payable (monies owed), taxes owed, accrued expenses, the current portion of long-term debt
- *Long-term liabilities:* notes that are due after one year (less the current portion)
- *Deferred taxes*: recognition of future tax consequences attributable to the differences between the financial statement, which carries the amounts of existing assets and liabilities, and the tax bases, operating loss and tax credit carry forwards.
- *Stockholders' equity:* the value of the securities issued and outstanding, additional paid-in capital, retained earnings

From the sum of these items the balance sheet states the "Total Liabilities" and the "Stockholders' Equity." And naturally, if properly drawn, the balance sheet will balance, reflecting the basic formula of a modern company. Reduced to its bare bones, the balance sheet should supply the following:

$$Assets = Liabilities + Capital$$
$$or$$
$$Capital = Assets - Liabilities$$

Clearly, the balance sheet indicates the value of the company; the net worth of the firm is nothing more than total assets minus total liabilities. And to take it one step further, the book value or stockholders' equity per share is the net worth of the company divided by the number of shares outstanding.

While the presentation of the balance sheet is uniformly consistent from company to company, the substance may not be. It is a question of what lies behind the figures. For instance, inventory valuation may be based on an FIFO (first in, first out) or LIFO (last in, first out) approach, the latter being more conservative than the former in an inflationary period. Both procedures are accepted by auditors, though the latter is open to interpretation: A conservative company will be cautious in putting a price on these intangible assets. Such caution may actually hide value. How much is the plant, property and equipment really worth? Is the figure based on original price or on replacement value? Sometimes the balance sheet can conceal as much as it reveals.

The balance sheet is followed by the statement of operations, also called the "income statement" or the "profit and loss" (P&L) statement. While the balance sheet tries to put a price tag on the company, the income statement measures the earnings and profitability of the business during the past year. The statement will start with revenues; move on to costs and expenses, additional income, taxes and extraordinary credits; subtract income taxes; and finally arrive at new income. This final figure will be divided by the number of shares outstanding to arrive at earnings per share.

As on the balance sheet, some of the items in the P&L statement are open to interpretation or conditioned by trade practice. Are sales for cash on the barrelhead, or, if not, how are credit sales handled? Are research and development costs capitalized over time or written off immediately? There is plenty of room for interpretation within "generally accepted accounting principles."

While the notes to the annual report sometimes hold the key, frequently Form 10K must be consulted for more precise explanations.

The consolidated statement or stockholders' equity summarizes changes in the equity capitalization, usually for a three-year period. It adds up the issuance of common stock, the exercise of warrants and options (the right to buy shares at a fixed price within a certain period), stock dividends, employees' stock ownership plans, any other paid-in capital and retained earnings. This overview tells stockholders how the owners' assets have grown (or shrunk) and how quickly.

The final statement—of change in financial position—reveals how the business uses its monies. Sources of funds are listed for the three-year period: net income, depreciation and amortization, increase in long-term debt, issuance of common stock. From these sources are subtracted the application of funds, or how the monies are used: new property, plant and equipment; reduction in long-term debt; conversion of debentures; stock purchased for treasury. What remains is the increase (or decrease) in working capital. The components of working capital have changed in the course of the year; this new mix of current assets and liabilities is then spelled out.

Finally, there is the auditor's report, which says, in effect, that the previous statements were prepared "in accordance with generally accepted auditing standards." Moreover, they reflect "fairly the financial position" of the company. Most auditors' statements are no more than three standard paragraphs long. A fourth paragraph should be a red flag to a prospective investor.

The Statements Explained

The previous statements—balance sheet, income or P&L statement, stockholders' equity, and changes in financial position—all speak for themselves. They allow direct year-to-year comparisons, indicating whether sales are up or down and by what percentages; whether earnings have kept pace with sales; and whether stockholders' equity is improving at a satisfactory rate. All are important and immediately obvious from these reports.

However, modern security analysis goes beyond the obvious data by asking for comparisons and ratios. These reveal not only how the company is doing but how well it is using its resources and how well it is managing its finances. There are half a dozen or so ratios that disclose the true underlying strengths of a business and enable one to compare the business with similar firms. These key ratios are:

1. Return on equity
2. Return on investment
3. Profit margin
4. Current ratio
5. Capitalization: debt versus equity

6. Cash flow
7. Earnings per share

But before arriving at these key ratios, one must examine the statements in the annual report. After a few years of successful operation, the Widget Works accounts may well look like those in Figure 1.1 on pages 20-21. The key ratios can now be derived from these basic documents.

Return on Equity

Return on equity is an indication of how productive stockholders' equity or property is at earning a profit. If management is efficient, effective and cost conscious, the return on equity will be high, and vice versa. Company equity consists of two items: the paid-in capital, or monies received for the sale of stock, and earnings retained and reinvested in the business. The return on equity can be calculated by dividing net income (from the statements of income) by stockholders' equity (from the balance sheets).

In the case of Widget Works Corporation:

$$\frac{\text{Net income}}{\text{Stockholders' equity}} = \frac{\$985,000}{\$3,125,000} = .3152 \text{ or } 31.52\%$$

The same result obtains by dividing earnings per share by book value (assets, less liabilities, divided by the number of shares outstanding):

$$\frac{\text{Earnings per share}}{\text{Book value}} = \frac{\$3.94}{\$12.50} = .3152$$

Companies that have a return on equity of 10 percent or less are, as a rule, less productive with their assets than the average. Companies with 20 percent or more are superbly managed. By itself, the figure is an excellent indication of how well the assets are being deployed. However, it is even more meaningful when compared with the returns of other companies in the same industry.

Return on Investment

Return on investment is a somewhat broader measure than return on equity, encompassing as it does all the resources of the company—both debt and equity. In fact, many observers find the return on investment one of the most critical of all financial yardsticks. In its long form, return on investment equals:

$$\frac{\text{Earnings}}{\text{Net sales}} \times \frac{\text{Net sales}}{\text{Total assets}}$$

For the Widget Works Corporation:

$$\frac{985,000}{6,500,000} \times \frac{6,500,000}{6,295,000} = .1564733 = 15.6\%$$

In the short form:

$$\frac{\text{Earnings}}{\text{Total assets}} = \frac{985,000}{6,295,000} = .1564733 = 15.6\%$$

In comparing return on investment, remember that earnings and total assets are sometimes defined differently from company to company. Earnings are commonly thought of as profit, but some companies use cash flow—or net profit after taxes, plus depreciation, depletion and other paper expenses. Assets are sometimes taken at their original book value, sometimes at their replacement cost. For consistency's sake, companies usually use earnings before taxes, sales after returns and allowances for bad debts, and book value of assets at the end of the year.

Return on investment analysis enables the investor to judge how well management is performing. Two companies can have roughly similar sales. But a look at return on investment could reveal that one company needed considerably more investment capital to achieve similar sales and profits.

FIGURE 1.1   Widget Works Corporation

Balance Sheets

ASSETS		
Current Assets		
Cash (including marketable securities)	$650,000	
Accounts Receivable	1,550,000	
Inventories		
Raw Materials	400,000	
Work in Process	870,000	
Finished Goods	200,000	
	1,470,000	
Total Current Assets		$3,670,000
Long-Term Assets		
Property, Plant & Equipment	2,500,000	
Other Assets	125,000	
Total Long-Term Assets		$2,625,000
Total Assets		$6,295,000

LIABILITIES AND STOCKHOLDERS' EQUITY		
Current Liabilities		
Notes and Loans Payable to Bank	$175,000	
Accounts Payable	490,000	
Accrued Expenses	530,000	
Income Taxes	55,000	
Other Current Liabilities	120,000	
Total Current Liabilities		$1,370,000
Long-Term Debt		$1,800,000
Stockholders' Equity		
Common Stock		
Authorized Shares—1,000,000		
Issued & Outstanding—250,000	1,500,000	
Additional Paid-in Capital	750,000	
Retained Earnings	875,000	
	1,625,000	
Total Stockholders' Equity		$3,125,000
Total Liabilities & Equity		$6,295,000

Statements of Income
(Year ended December 31)

REVENUES	
Net Sales	$6,500,000
Interest & Royalty Income	250,000
Legal Settlement	110,000
Total Revenues	$6,860,000
COST & EXPENSES	
Cost of Products Sold	$4,250,000
Research & Development	650,000
Selling, General and Administrative Expenses	600,000
Depreciation	50,000
Interest	25,000
Total Cost & Expenses	$5,575,000
INCOME BEFORE TAXES	$1,285,000
INCOME TAXES	300,000
NET INCOME	$985,000
INCOME PER COMMON SHARE (250,000 shares outstanding)	$3.94

Statements of Changes in Financial Position

Source of Funds	
Net Income	$985,000
Depreciation & Amortization	50,000
Total from Operations	$1,035,000
Increase in Long-Term Debt	100,000
Issuance of Shares	
Officers and Directors	5,000
Proceeds from Employees' Stock Option Plan	5,000
Proceeds from Properties Sold	100,000
Total from Nonoperating Sources	$210,000
Total	$1,245,000
Application of Funds	
Additions to Property, Plant & Equipment	725,000
Reduction in Long-Term Debt	80,000
Conversion of Debentures	135,000
Cash Dividends Paid Out	125,000
Total	$1,065,000
Increase in Working Capital	$180,000

Profit Margin

A company's profit margin, obtained from the income statements, is another litmus test of how productive it is with regard to its revenues. Obviously, a company making a penny on a dollar of sales is less profitable than one making a dime on a dollar of sales. Net profits on net sales is obtained by dividing net earnings, or profits after taxes, by net sales.

For the Widget Works Corporation:

$$\frac{\text{Earnings}}{\text{Net sales}} = \frac{985,000}{6,500,000} = .1515384 = 15\%$$

Again, there is marked difference from industry to industry. In the retail trade, the lowest profit margins are typically found in grocery stores—little more than 1 percent. In manufacturing, among the highest is bottled and canned soft drinks. Both are rather pedestrian, commonplace product lines. But as might be expected, the shares of the former group have one of the lowest price-earnings ratios, while the latter group has some of the highest.

Current Ratio

The current ratio derived from the balance sheets is an important indicator, not of corporate profitability but of corporate strength. It reveals the degree of safety of an investment, whether the company has enough fat on its bones to weather a severe downturn in its business or a national recession. The current ratio is arrived at by dividing current assets by current liabilities.

For the Widget Works Corporation:

$$\frac{\text{Current assets}}{\text{Current liabilities}} = \frac{3,670,000}{1,370,000} = 2.67\%$$

A current ratio of two—meaning that there are $2 of assets to meet every $1 of current debt—is usually felt to ensure a margin of safety for most manufacturing companies. However, financial organizations, utilities and service-oriented businesses may have lower current ratios. If the ratio is much above 3, it suggests that a conservative management is not using its resources as effectively as it could be.

It is also a flag for the acquisition-minded, indicating unemployed assets and perhaps a pot of gold. This ratio can be sharpened even further by applying the "acid test" or "quick ratio": Only the cash and equivalents are used in the current ratio. This acid test is extreme, a test of solvency if the company is on the ropes.

Capital Structure

A company's capital structure is indicative of the financial management's conservative or liberal attitudes. A conservatively managed company will have little or no debt; conversely, one with a large debt has a liberal attitude toward risk. (Some businesses, such as finance, real estate and utility companies, incur considerable debt by the nature of their enterprise.) However, conservative versus liberal management is not necessarily good. A conservatively managed company may not know how to use borrowed money; perhaps it would be more profitable if it did. A liberally managed company, on the other hand, may be taking advantage of the leverage connected with borrowing, but may not realize that it is also putting its equity owners in jeopardy.

In recent years, industrial companies have borrowed a great deal more money than they used to. A company that borrows 50 percent (or more) of its capitalization is said to be highly leveraged. In the Widget Works Corporation:

$$\frac{\text{Long-term debt}}{\text{Stockholders' equity}} = \frac{1,800,000}{3,125,000} = .58$$

Thus, the debt-equity ratio is:

$$\frac{\text{Long-term debt} = 58\%}{\text{Stockholders' equity} = 42\%}$$

The Widget Works, as a young, rapidly expanding company, is highly leveraged and therefore a risky investment at this stage of its growth. As companies mature, they tend to use less debt in their capitalization. In England, leverage is called "gearing," and its effects have been summed up in a ditty that is universally applicable:

> The higher the gearing, the faster the pace.
> The lower the gearing, the less to face.

Cash Flow

Increasingly, cash flow is looked upon as a sign of financial health, the company's ability to perpetuate itself. Cash flow is the net income plus the depreciation, amortization, depletion and other extraordinary charges to revenues that are deductions but are not paid out of the income statement in real dollars. Thus cash flow is a better indicator than net income of funds for internal capital expenditures and dividends.

For the Widget Works Corporation:

$$\text{Cash flow} = \text{Net income} + \text{Depreciation}$$
$$\$1,035,000 = \$985,000 + \$50,000$$

Older companies usually have higher cash flows due to the magnitude of depreciation (in some instances, new tax laws have accelerated that depreciation). In addition, cash flow is augmented by how rapidly the inventory or product line turns over in the course of a year.

Earnings per Share

Earnings per share, probably the single most observed statistic for investors, is a summary of the earning ability of the company's equity. It is arrived at by dividing the net earnings (after taxes) by the number of shares outstanding. There are two ways of looking at earnings per share. The figure expressed in the daily stock listing reflects the last 12 months of earnings—lagging earnings. While important in ascertaining a trend and making comparisons, especially from quarterly period to quarterly period, this figure has little predictive value. More attention is paid to projected or estimated earnings. Some companies, with the implied sanction of the SEC, make tentative estimates of business and earnings for a quarter or a year ahead. Brokerage houses, financial newsletters, magazines and investment counselors also make their own projections.

CHAPTER 2

Corporate Bonds

An honest man's word is as good as his bond.

—Cervantes

Why a Debt Market

Bonds may well be the least understood financial instruments in the world of securities. This is a bit of a paradox, since in terms of volume and dollars, trading in bonds far outweighs trading in shares. Nevertheless, the public has shied away from the bond market, viewing it as an enclave reserved for professional traders, money managers and bankers.

In its wisdom, the public may be right. A sound rule of thumb is: If you can't understand it, don't invest in it. Public hesitancy may also come from the simple fact that in an inflationary era, when depreciation of the currency is the order of the day, a fixed, long-term obligation is not the thing to own. Every high school economics text asserts that during inflation it is better to be a borrower and to pay back the loan with "cheap" money, rather than a lender, who will recover his funds only years later, when they will have lost some or much of their purchasing power.

Certainly, the 1970s and early 1980s were a period of significant inflation. Indeed, the period was marked by a couple of dollar crises and devaluations, the unleashing of gold, soaring petroleum prices, and a universal rush from currencies to collectibles. For a variety of reasons, then, bonds were the great underachievers. Every year the investment banking house of Salomon Brothers ranks investments against the consumer price index (CPI). The compound annual rates of return for major categories of investments for the past decade rank as follows:

1.	Emerging Market Equity	21.3%
2.	EAFE	17.5
3.	Japanese Stocks	16.2
4.	S&P 500	15.0
5.	U.S. Treasury Long Bonds	14.3
6.	Corporate Bonds	13.8
7.	Junk Bonds	13.8
8.	Art	12.2
9.	Emerging Growth Stocks	11.4
10.	Intermediate-Term Govt. Bonds	11.1
11.	Venture Capital	7.5
12.	Commercial Paper	7.0
13.	T-Bills	6.4
14.	U.S. Farmland	4.7
15.	Residential Housing	4.4
16.	Foreign Bonds	4.1
17.	Commercial Real Estate	3.9
18.	Inflation	3.7

Source: Barron's; EAFE-Europe, Asia, Far East Index. All returns are for the period ended December 31, 1993.

In the last few years, many of the conceptions about bonds have undergone substantial change, and they are no longer the province of financial sophisticates and professionals. The general public has gotten in on the act by trading them for capital gains, investing in them for higher yields and buying them for tax-free income. Before looking at some of the current practices, a review of bonds and the bond markets is appropriate.

Whereas equity shares represent ownership of a company, bonds represent debts of a company, and bondholders, in effect, are creditors. It is possible for a business to borrow on a short-term basis to finance its daily, weekly or seasonal business. Such short-term lending by a bank or other financial organization is usually based on the track record of the company, its ability to repay the loan out of current proceeds and sometimes by taking title to the accounts receivable.

But long-term growth cannot be based on this type of financing. Plant, equipment, real estate, transportation equipment and all the other major components that go into building up a company must be paid for up front, but may not pay back or return their investment for many years. Moreover, the cost of such capital expenditures is quite large—usually beyond the means of one lender or one source of funds. Clearly, long-term debt is the answer.

The traditional way of borrowing money for long periods of time—usually somewhere between 5 and 30 years—is to issue corporate bonds. There are many variations, but they are all formal, legal IOUs. With corporate bonds sold to the public (as opposed to a private placement, where the lender is a financial institution or knowledgeable investor), the following four parties are usually involved in the sale:

1. The issuer or debtor—the business borrowing the funds
2. A legal firm, which issues the trust indenture or promissory note (an integral part of every bond certificate, which sets forth the maturity date, interest rate, security and other terms)
3. The corporate trustee—a bank or trust company, which authenticates the bond's issuance, facilitates its transfer and protects the rights of the bondholder
4. The bondholder or creditor—the individual or company lending the money

Bonds are usually sold in $1,000 denominations—that is, the par value (or face value) is $1,000. Unlike stock prices, which are fully quoted, bond prices are given as percentages of 1,000—with a zero missing, so to speak. Therefore, a bond that is quoted at 87 is really selling for $870. Whereas a point in the stock market is $1, a point in the bond market is $10. Corporate bonds are quoted in fractions of a point—usually in eighths, as in the equities markets—but one point is $10 and one-eighth is $1.25. Thus, if the bond at 87 sold off by 1⅜, $13.75, the new price would be 85⅝, or $856.25.

Among the important rights secured by the indenture is the right to be paid the full face value of the bond when it matures, or falls due, and to be paid interest every six months. The interest rate is also stated on the bond, an 8-by-10-inch engraved certificate. If the interest rate is 10 percent, or $100, then every six months the owner of the bond will be paid half the interest, or $50. In the daily press, the quotation would look like this:

Bonds	Cur Yld	Vol	High	Low	Close	Net Chg
WiW 10s06	11.6	9	87	85⅜	85⅝	−1⅜

Yesterday, Widget Works 10 percent bonds maturing in the year 2006 (see the first column) were selling at a current yield of 11.6 percent; nine bonds were traded, with the high for the day at 87 ($870), the low at 85⅜ ($856.25), where it closed, off 1⅜ ($13.75).

Although the $1,000 face value is by far the most common, bonds do come in different denominations. They also come in two distinct forms, which determine how the bondholder is paid. Coupon bonds have a series of coupons attached to them that must be clipped off and presented to a bank or brokerage house for collection. Coupon bonds are usually bearer bonds, meaning that they are not registered to any owner, but are owned by whoever possesses them.

On the other hand, registered bonds usually have no coupons; the corporation's transfer agent keeps track of who owns the bond and sends the interest payment automatically. Ownership is determined not by possession but by whose name is carried on the company's books. Today, most bonds are issued in registered form to protect the bondholder from theft, loss or forgery. (Municipalities used to issue bearer securities but are now obliged to issue only registered bonds.) To purchasers of bonds who leave them with their brokers, the distinction is academic, since their ownership is vouchsafed by a bookkeeping entry on their monthly statement.

When a corporation sells an initial bond offering—usually through an underwriting syndicate made up of several investment banking houses—an announcement is made in the press through a tombstone advertisement. This is a bare note indicating only the company name, the underwriters, the amount being borrowed, the price, the date(s) the issue(s) matures and the interest rate. The face value of the bond remains constant: It is issued at $1,000 and is redeemed at the end of its life for the same amount. The only thing subject to change during the bond's life is its selling price. Conversely, the interest rate it originally promised to pay will remain constant. These two factors—price and interest rate—play against each other in the open market.

Face Value and Interest Rates

The deciding factor in the price of a bond, besides supply and demand, is the prevailing interest rate. For example, if the original bond issue had a coupon rate of 10 percent, when general interest rates rise the price of the bond will fall. Should interest rates rise so that a new, comparable bond issue would have to pay an 11 percent rate, the old bond price would fall so that its 10 percent rate would yield 11 percent:

$$\$100 \div 11\% = \$909$$

At $909, a 10 percent interest rate has a current yield of 11 percent, thus making the old bond competitive with the new one, all other things being equal. On the other hand, should interest rates fall so that a new, comparable bond issue need pay only a 9 percent rate, the old bond price would rise so that its 10 percent rate could yield 9 percent:

$$\$100 \div 9\% = \$1,111$$

At $1,111, a 10 percent interest rate has a current yield of 9 percent, again making the old and new bonds competitive as both prices hover about the prevailing interest rates for bonds of their respective quality. These two examples—of a bond selling at a discount from its original face value and a bond selling at a premium—reflect the usual behavior of bond prices in response to interest rates. This key relationship is best remembered by thinking of the two as sitting on opposite sides of a seesaw: When bond prices decline, the current yield goes up; when the interest rate goes down, bond prices rise. Thus the current yield is determined by these two factors.

But bonds are, of course, investments over a period of time. Bondholders are interested in the current yield, but perhaps more important, they are interested in the yield to maturity. If a bond is bought at the initial offering and held throughout its life, the yield to maturity need not be considered since it is the same as the current yield or coupon rate. And many bondholders do buy at the offering and put the bonds away.

However, there is a broad and active secondary market in most corporate bonds. When bonds are sold at other than their face value, either at a discount or at a premium, that difference must be figured in to arrive at the bond's final value when it is redeemed. A bond purchased at a premium will lose value as its due date approaches, and its yield to maturity will be less than its current yield. When there is a loss of principal on a bond bought at a premium, the investor is entitled to a capital loss for tax purposes. When there is a gain in principal from a discounted bond, the investor must report that as a capital gain.

The mathematics involved in calculating the yield to maturity are not so much difficult as time consuming. Consequently, before the computer era, bond tables indicated the value of a bond with various coupon rates and maturity dates. Today, computers and programmable calculators can come up with the present value of a bond or the yield to maturity in a nanosecond.

Quality Ratings

Clearly, the maturity date is one of the determinants of a bond's value and the coupon rate is another; both are stated on the face of the bond certificate. Equally important, though not stated on the certificate, is the bond's quality.

Bond quality is a measurement of many factors: the corporation's earning power, the strength of its assets, the relationship of assets to liabilities, the amount of debt previously incurred and the ratio of debt to equity, as well as other variables such as the industry and the state of the economy. Obviously, with so many variables to consider, rating the quality of a bond is a complex job, best left to professionals. The two major rating services relied upon by the financial world are Moody's Investors Service and Standard & Poor's Corporation. After analyzing all the factors, these services assign letter grades. In descending order of quality, they are:

Moody's	Standard & Poor's
Aaa	AAA
Aa	AA (+ –)
A	A (+ –)
Baa	BBB (+ –)
Ba	BB (+ –)
B	B (+ –)
Caa	CCC
	D

In general, bonds in the top two A categories are prudent investments for banks, fiduciaries, and others charged with the paramount safety of other people's money. The single A category and the first class of B bonds are of medium investment grade but lack protection in the event of a business downturn. Anything less—Ba, BB(+ –), B, B(+ –)—is speculative, lacking the protective elements necessary for investment quality. Finally, C and D bonds are either close to or in default; they have ceased to pay interest and/or are in arrears in redeeming the principal.

The nuances between bond categories, between a triple A and a double A, for instance, are hard to appreciate. When the nuances are reduced to differences in yields it becomes clearer. For example, over the past few years the difference in yield between triple A and double A has averaged about a quarter of a percentage point. (In the bond world, a percentage point consists of 100 basis points. Thus, a quarter of a percentage point is 25 basis points.) And the difference between triple A and triple B is usually more than 1 whole point (100 basis points).

Bond ratings are an attempt to quantify the degree of risk involved in the ownership of different debt obligations. They are one response to a simple truth: When it comes to lending money, both individuals and institutions tend to shy away from risk, preferring stability to chance. Consequently, for lenders to take on risk, they must be rewarded by higher returns. In the case of bonds, the yields in the more speculative issues must be commensurate with the increased chance of default and bankruptcy. In short, the greater the risk an issue carries, the greater the reward that must accompany the investment. Historically, low-grade bonds have had higher rates of return than high-grade bonds.

Most bond buyers are very conscious about the rate of return and the yield to maturity of their holdings. One unpredictable factor sometimes throws off their calculations: the call element; many bonds have call protection fixed in their indenture. The corporation is borrowing money at a fixed rate of interest over a long period. If the coupon rate is 10 percent and that remains the going rate for comparable issues over the life of the bond, both the borrower and the lender will feel content. However, this rarely happens. A prolonged period of inflation pushing interest rates up will certainly discomfort lenders as they see the price of their holdings fall and the value of their money depreciate upon maturity of the bond. Bondholders may, of course, sell their bond if they foresee a prolonged period of inflation, and move their assets to some other investment that will weather the storm.

On the other hand, should the economy undergo a prolonged deflation and interest rates fall so that comparable bond issues can be floated at 5 percent, it is the borrowing corporation that will feel discomforted. Instead of continuing to pay such high rates, the issuer will take advantage of a provision in the indenture to call in all or part of that bond series.

Bonds that afford the issuer such protection have something for the lender as well: Such bonds are not usually callable for the first five or ten years of their life, and if they are called, the holder receives not only the face value but a small percentage over par—2 percent, 3 percent or 5 percent—depending upon which year they are redeemed. The issuing company can turn around and issue a new series of bonds at the new prevailing rate of 5 percent and save considerable interest costs. Bonds that are not redeemed cease to accrue interest, so nothing is gained by not surrendering the certificates.

The Bond Universe

There is a universe of bonds—a kind for every type of financing imaginable. From the corporate treasurer's point of view, bond financing has one great advantage over equity financing under the present tax laws. Interest charges must be paid to bondholders, whether or not the company earns any profit for the year. Dividends to the stockholders are arbitrary, decided upon by the board of directors. On the surface, it would appear that bond financing ties the company into a fixed charge, regardless of business conditions, while stock issues and subsequent dividends have a direct relationship to what the company can afford. However, companies that wish to build stockholders' loyalty, an institutional following and a continuous record of dividend payments find themselves tied almost as tightly to those dividend payments as they would be to bond interest payments.

Under the tax code, interest payments for debt are deductible business expenses against revenues. Dividend payments are not. Dividends can only be paid against net earnings—that is, earnings after taxes. The difference is significant, and many treasurers consider bond financing "cheaper" than issuing stock, which could require dividend payments and in addition would dilute the equity.

For the established corporation, the most common bond issue is a debenture, a promissory note backed by a corporation's general credit rather than by any tangible, specific collateral. Debenture bonds are issued by large, mainstream corporations. If Shylock in Shakespeare's *Merchant of Venice* had lent money against a debenture, he would have had no particular physical claim.

But Shylock lent 3,000 ducats to Antonio on a mortgage bond; in return, he pledged a pound of flesh. Modern bondholders are less sanguinary in their demands but just as skeptical about being paid back their principal. Their demand is usually spelled out in mortgage bonds, where corporate assets are pledged against the borrowed sum. Occasionally, mortgage bonds are issued in series, each issue being backed by some of the company's property. In case of default, the mortgaged property is subject to sale so that bondholders can recover their funds. In practice, financial reorganizations are carried out under the protection of the court in an attempt to salvage, not sell, the corporate business. But the mortgage lien certainly puts the bondholder in a strategic position as a creditor with a prior claim to influence the bankruptcy proceedings.

Mortgage bonds are a favorite of utilities, and debentures are the usual tools of manufacturing companies. In general, holders of debentures have all the privileges of creditors on assets that are not otherwise or previously pledged. Consequently, these unsecured bonds usually yield somewhat higher rates than mortgage bonds. Though there may be no specific pledge of corporate property, debenture indentures usually give some bondholder protection by limiting the amount of debt, requiring ample working capital or limiting dividend payments.

Equipment trust certificates (ETCs) are another option in the bond market. Traditionally these were a form of mortgage bond, but the underlying equipment was the rolling stock of railroad companies. This was excellent collateral since it could be used by any railroad in any part of the country. A trust was established to enable a trustee to buy cars from a manufacturer, and these were in turn leased to a railroad on a rental basis. The trustee would sell these ETCs to the public, who received the rents. When the railroad had completed its lease payments, usually within 10 or 15 years, the railroad would take legal possession of the cars and the certificate holders were paid off. During the Great Depression railroads paid off on their ETCs, though not always on their mortgage bonds. Thus ETCs have had an excellent reputation and have been used to finance other forms of transportation, from airlines to oil tankers. ETCs have complete call protection, too, since there is no feature allowing for their early redemption.

Finally, there are convertible bonds, debentures that some investors regard as attractive hybrids that give the best of both worlds. But no financial instrument offers something for nothing, a warning that is particularly true of convertibles. Unlike other securities, convertible bonds offer two distinct ways of winning—but there are two distinct ways of losing with them as well.

Convertible bonds are offered by corporations that would like to raise money without paying exorbitant interest rates, at the same time postponing the dilution of the equity until earnings are better. Convertible debentures are a happy compromise since they usually require lower rates than straight bonds, but more than dividends on comparable equity. The issue provides for an exchange of bonds for a set number of shares. For instance, a $1,000 bond is convertible into so many common shares of the issuing company at $20; this is known as the "conversion ratio" or "rate of the bond."

The conversion ratio is fixed when the convertible bond is issued—usually at a value above the current market value of the common stock. In this case the new issue has a conversion parity price of $20 ($1,000 ÷ 50 = $20), while the current market price is $15. At $15, the convertible bond's conversion value is worth $750. An exchange at this point would make no sense, for the investor would be left with 50 shares worth only $15 per share. Conversion becomes valuable only when the price of the common stock rises above this conversion price. When the common is at $25, the bond is then worth $1,250 (50 × $25). Once above the conversion ratio, the convertible bond and the common stock should move in lockstep.

Since there is an active secondary market in convertibles, it is possible to buy them at premiums, or discounts from par. The price of convertible bonds in the open market depends partially on the relation of common to convertible and partially on the coupon rate of the bond. The investment value of a convertible can also be appreciated by looking at it as a straight bond and calculating its yield to maturity. As a straight bond, the investment value is clearly less than as a convertible since it has no kicker or sweetener. Because of its yield, convertible bonds have a floor under them; that floor, or price support, consists of the prevailing interest rates for issues of comparable value.

Though the investment value—that is, its yield to maturity—may appear to give the convertible a floor, it is possible to have the worst of both worlds: On the bond side, interest rates may rise in general and the price of bonds fall, while on the equity side, the price of the common falls. The good news is that both elements can work positively: Interest rates may fall and bonds appreciate while common stock also heads north.

This two-sided character of convertibles has been viewed as a "conservative's way to speculate." Bear in mind that if the common is not more than 20 percent below the conversion price and that as a straight bond the convertible would not be more than 20 percent below its present price, the potential is pleasing if the company is in good shape and its business prospects are good. In the last analysis, a convertible bond is a hybrid, giving the purchaser a call on the underlying common for a somewhat lower yield.

The Markets for Bonds

In a small, quiet room off the trading floor of the New York Stock Exchange, the "bond crowd" goes about its business. Stocks on the Big Board trade something on the order of 70 billion shares annually, whereas the bond volume is only $10 billion of par value. But there are more bond issues than stock issues listed on the NYSE.

Corporate bonds are also traded on the American Stock Exchange; most are bonds of companies listed on the AMEX. As with equity trading, bond trading on both exchanges is based on the auction system. Specialists make a market and trade as few as one bond, though some brokers are reluctant to trade small lots since the commission rate is so unprofitable that it barely covers the paperwork. The auction market is especially sensitive to supply and demand pressures. Prices on inactive bonds can show sizable daily changes and the spread can be quite wide. The two exchanges trade not only the straight bonds but also convertibles. After the straight bond listing are noted the current yield, the volume and the daily changes. After the convertible there is no current yield, only a cv to indicate its convertible nature; this so affects its current yield as to make comparative use of that information pointless. Therefore, it is omitted.

A greater number of publicly traded corporate bonds are available in the OTC market. Here the market is maintained by dealers, a few dozen bond houses that trade for their own account. As with stocks, prices are negotiated; and instead of paying a broker's commission, the purchaser is dealt with on a net basis. The dealer profits by the spread—the difference between what he or she paid and what he or she sells the merchandise for. Since there may be many dealers for a given issue, the competition holds the markup or markdown to a slim margin. Bond dealers primarily trade among themselves and institutions, but also with broker-dealers, who in turn sell on a retail basis to individual customers.

Bonds, whether traded on the exchanges or in the OTC market, are traded with interest. The purchaser agrees to pay the principal sum, plus whatever interest has accrued from the last payment. Some bonds are traded flat; these are designated by an f in the current yield column. Such bonds are in default or have some problem that prohibits them from complying with their next interest payment.

CHAPTER 3

U.S. Government Debt and Municipals

A national debt, if it is not excessive, will be to us a national blessing.

—Alexander Hamilton

Blessed are the young, for they shall inherit the national debt.

—Herbert Hoover

Federal Paper

In 1982, the federal government passed a mind-boggling milestone: The national debt exceeded the trillion-dollar mark. Except for a couple of years in the mid-1830s, the U.S. government has always been in debt. Today, however, interest on the national debt is the fourth largest item in the federal budget, and for the last few years, federal budget deficits have been on the order of $200 billion. The 1994 American national elections were to some degree fought over the current deficit and the national debt. With the Republican party winning those elections, promises were made to balance the budget by the year 2002. Debt is an issue that stirs great emotions since it is a generational transfer of wealth, without future generations having any representation at the table.

On the other hand, America's national debt is smaller in terms of the GNP than that of some other major industrial countries, including Japan and Germany. To many people, the magnitude of government debt is cause for concern. But others feel that debt itself is not cause for worry; what matters is not the ability to repay the debt but the ability to maintain payments on the interest.

There may be truth in both views, but for the purchaser of federal government debt securities, the chief concern must be with the latter. And thus far the federal government has always paid interest and principal on its obligations—on time and without a hassle. Government paper is backed by the full faith and credit of the national government. To put it more directly, government paper is backed by the federal government's power to tax. Since no one seriously questions the government's ability or intention to refund and/or refinance its debt as each issue comes due, its bills, notes and bonds are considered the safest investment.

American debt obligations are thought of as a financial haven all over the world, not only for private holdings but as a reserve currency for foreign central banks. Alexander Hamilton helped to establish American credit in the 18th century, and though the government's credibility has occasionally been shaken, its financial creditworthiness has never been questioned. Hamilton is buried at the foot of Wall Street, with good reason.

More than half of the government debt is marketable debt, or debt instruments that are actively traded after their initial sale to the public. The other portion of the total debt consists of issues sold to foreign central banks, federal agencies, trust funds and plus E and H series savings bonds. There is no secondary market in these issues. Government obligations come in three groups, classified by when they fall due. Bonds are the longest-term debt, maturing between 10 and 30 years from their date of issue. The Treasury's longest maturity are 30-year bonds; for example, the $7 ⅝s of 2025. Treasury notes have maturities between 1 year and 7 or 10 years; like bonds, they are available in denominations of $1,000 and pay interest semiannually. Treasury bills are short-term securities, with maturities of 13 weeks, 26 weeks or 1 year.

Since government paper is not rated by the rating services, the differences have to do with length of maturities and yields. Daily price fluctuations of government securities are minimal. Indeed, while the corporate bond market moves in increments of ⅛ point ($1.25 per $1,000 bond), the price of Treasury securities usually moves in increments of ¹⁄₃₂

($.03125) and sometimes of ⅟₆₄ point ($.015625). Thus a bid quotation of "97.6" means $971.875; the ask quotation of "97.10" means $973.125.

The notation under "Treasury Bills, Bonds and Notes" in the press for the previously mentioned 30-year bond looks like this:

Date	Rate	Bid	Asked	Change	Yield
2-25	7 ⅞s	102.19	102.23	−31	7.40

Unlike some foreign countries, the United States does not have open-ended or unredeemable debt. The most famous examples of this kind are the British Consols, which were first sold in 1750. They pay interest and sell only on a current-yield basis since there is no likelihood that they will ever be called.

Treasury bills (T-bills) are sold for less than their face value but are redeemed at their face value on maturity; in other words, the interest is paid up front. The discount equals the interest rate, which is set by weekly competitive bidding. The individual investor pays what amounts to the average price of the accepted competitive bids. Sold in minimum denominations of $10,000, Treasury bills can be purchased directly from any Federal Reserve Bank or through a bank or brokerage house for a small service charge. They are now issued only in registered, book-entry form.

Long-term Treasury bonds are issued in either registered or bearer form, but unlike notes or bills, some have a call provision that enables the government to call in the obligation five years before it matures. This feature in some long-term bonds makes any projection of the bond's future income stream somewhat unpredictable.

U.S. government obligations are priced according to their yield, which is determined by the actual coupon yield (or discount, in the case of T-bills), the maturity date and market conditions. Since all debt issues of the Treasury are of the highest quality with regard to safety of principal and payment of interest, they generally offer somewhat lower yields than other securities with comparable maturities. Current yield is closely related to prevailing interest rates and maturity. Long-term bonds tend to have the highest current yields, reflecting the greater uncertainty of future events. That uncertainty is compensated for, as it were, by higher interest rates. For example, in 1995 the differences in interest rates were:

3-month T-bills	5.64%
6-month T-bills	5.50%
3-year Treasury Notes	6.81%
10-year Treasury Notes	7.11%
30-year Bonds	7.37%

Since the late 1970s, interest rates have fluctuated widely and wildly, with significant changes occurring not only week to week but even daily. For individuals, these sharp fluctuations sometimes make purchases in the after market more profitable than new issues bought directly from the Treasury. Even though there may be a slight charge by the bank or brokerage house, the price fluctuations due to market conditions and the menu of dozens of different issues may offer the investor greater selection.

Finally, interest rates on federal government securities are conditioned by one other important factor. In addition to their being free of risk, the income from them is exempt from state and local income taxes, though it is subject to federal income taxes.

The quotation for one of the approximately two dozen Treasury bill issues in the financial press appears as follows:

Maturity Date	Bid	Asked	Change	Yield
3-07-96	6.00	5.97	+.10	6.34

Thus the 180-day T-bill (in denominations of $10,000 to $1 million) is selling for 6.00, or a yield of 6.34 percent on a discounted basis. The yields quoted are a percentage of the discount which is figured on an annual basis even though the bills have maturity dates of less than a year.

To calculate the discount on $10,000:

$$\text{Maturity (days)} \div 360 \times .0597 \times \$10,000$$
$$180 \div 360 \times .0597 \times \$10,000 = \$298.50$$

To calculate the price:

$$\$10,000 - \$298.50 = \$9,701.50$$

Due to the arithmetic employed, the discounted rate yields slightly more than the bond yield basis, which is used to calculate interest on time deposit in banks. Under "Treasury Bonds and Notes" in the press are listed roughly 150 issues maturing anywhere from tomorrow to the year 2025. A typical quotation looks as follows:

Coupon Rate	Maturity Date	Bid	Asked	Change	Yield
7 ⅞s	1-98	102.17	102.21	−.10	6.61

In the secondary market, the Treasury note of 1–1998, originally issued to yield 7.875 percent, is now being offered at 102.17, that is, 102.53125 or $1025.3125 per $1,000 of face value (since fractions are ½ point). The bond was down ten ticks (.10 × .03125) or $3.125 over the previous day. Most individual buyers and sellers of government bonds will never see the actual certificates since, increasingly, small transactions are completed by book entry. Unless there is some compelling legal reason to take possession of the note or bond, this procedure enhances safety, since in bearer form there is no record in case of loss.

Treasury issues can be bought from brokerage houses and banks for a small handling charge (about $50), or can be bought from a Federal Reserve branch without paying a commission through a program called Treasury Direct. The minimum denomination for Treasury bills is $10,000, plus multiples of $1,000. The 2-year and 3-year notes have a minimum denomination of $5,000, plus multiples of $1,000. The 5-year and 10-year notes and all Treasury bonds have a minimum denomination of $1,000, plus multiples of $1,000.

Treasury bills have 117 issues annually: 13- and 26-week bills are issued weekly; 52-week bills are issued every fourth week. Two-year and 5-year notes are issued at the end of each month; 3-year and 10-year notes are issued on the 15th of February, May, August and November. Thirty-year bonds are issued on the 15th of February and August.

Federal Agencies

The Treasury is not the only issuer of government debt obligations, though it is the largest. Over the years, 20 different agencies of the federal government have taken to issuing their own paper. While Treasury borrowings are used to finance the national deficits arising from the shortfalls in the budget, the agencies are financing loans in the form of mortgages or credits. The difference is significant, since the agencies hope to recover their loans eventually, a hope not shared by the Treasury, with its growing deficit.

Since these agency securities are not Treasury obligations, the agencies sweeten the pot by offering higher yields to attract investors. Another sweetener is the absence of a call; agency paper is not redeemable before it matures. Technically speaking, Treasury bonds, notes and bills are backed by the full faith and credit of the United States. Of all the agencies offering securities, only the Government National Mortgage Association (Ginnie Mae) and the Export-Import Bank (Eximbank) have that backing. All the other agencies have some kind of government approval—their securities may be approved by the Treasury, issued under an act of Congress, issued through the Federal Reserve Banks, or considered a legal investment for federally supervised institutions—but they do not carry a full faith clause.

The real question is: Does it make any difference? Historically, apparently not, but the case remains untried since none of these agencies have ever had a liquidity or insolvency problem. It seems highly unlikely that the federal government would ever let a financial crisis undermine the creditworthiness of any of these issues.

In the agricultural industry, the significant issues are from the Federal Land Bank, Federal Farm Credit, Federal Intermediate Credit Bank and the Bank for Coops. In the housing industry there are issues of the Federal Home Loan Bank, Federal National Mortgage Association and the Government National Mortgage Association. Finally, there are issues of the World Bank (International Bank for Reconstruction and Development), the Inter-American Development Bank and the Asian Development Bank. While they are all traded in a fashion similar to that of Treasury issues, some are exempt from state and local taxes.

Investors can purchase new Treasury issues, at the average price for accepted bids, directly from any of the 12 member banks of the Federal Reserve System. Not so with other government paper. Instead of holding an auction, these agencies have their securities underwritten by syndicates of investment bankers. A syndicate buys the new issue, sets a coupon rate, receives a sales commission and then retails the issue at par. Since there is an active secondary market, agency paper can be bought and sold quite easily; it is quoted in the press in a fashion similar to that of Treasury notes and bonds.

Agency bonds are not well known in the investment community, even though they have some of the highest yields of federally guaranteed paper and a variety of maturity dates. The Government National Mortgage Association is perhaps an exception. Since its inception as a separate corporation within the Department of Housing and Urban Development, Ginnie Mae has been responsible for making real estate investments more desirable to institutions by offering securities backed by pools of VA and FHA mortgages. These participation certificates, about a dozen issues, are traded in the secondary market in denominations of $5,000 and $10,000.

Ginnie Mae also developed and sells pass-through certificates in $25,000 denominations, which are backed by pools of residential mortgages assembled by private lenders. The payment of interest and principal by the mortgage holders is passed through to the certificate holders (after servicing fees). The certificates have maturity dates similar to the mortgages, but prepayment of mortgages is common, making the average close to 12 years. Prorated shares of principal and interest are distributed monthly. Similar pass-through certificates are issued by the Federal Home Loan Mortgage Corporation, the Federal National Mortgage Association (Fannie Mae), and the Student Loan Marketing Association (Sallie Mae), without a full faith and credit guarantee, in $10,000, $25,000 and $50,000 units. Fannie Mae is now a public company whose shares are listed on the NYSE, and shares of Sallie Mae are traded there also.

Another option are unit trusts of Ginnie Mae certificates, which offer shares to the public in $1,000 denominations. There is an active secondary market in all these mortgage-backed securities. While Ginnie Mae has a full faith and credit backing, unlike most of the other government agencies, it should be noted that this guarantee is against credit loss, not market risk. In other words, rates from these mortgage pools will continue to change and the returns will be sensitive to interest rates.

The Municipal Market

City, state and other authorities have not been far behind the federal government in issuing debt. These local issues—obligations of states, cities, political subdivisions, public authorities or any agencies legally empowered to issue nontaxable debt—are loosely and generally called municipals. This municipal market has virtually exploded in the last 15 years, now valued at $1.2 trillion. Seventy percent of all munis are held by individuals, a remarkable vote of confidence since only a decade ago that figure was only 45 percent.

There are a number of reasons why the markets for these securities expanded so quickly, but they are somewhat contradictory. One overriding condition was the reality of inflation: It pushed up wages, salaries and fee structures, inevitably causing higher levels of taxation as everyone was placed in a higher tax bracket. While some income could be sheltered through various investment devices, they were frequently speculative and finally were curtailed by the government in the 1970s. Municipals were the answer to fixed-interest, tax-sheltered investments since they were perfectly sound and legally reputable.

But a funny thing happened on the way to sheltering income via municipals. A number of municipal bond issues in New York, Ohio and Michigan fell into disrepute and developed full-fledged credibility crises. With the staggering interest rates of 1978 through 1981, the prices of outstanding bonds fell precipitously, if only on paper. Finally, a number of states, from California to Massachusetts, passed referendums limiting the taxing power of local governments, thus casting another shadow on municipal bond credibility.

Nevertheless, the underwriting and buying of municipal bonds goes on at record rates. And for very good reason: Next to issues of the U.S. government, municipals are one of the safest investments one can make. They are backed by the full faith and credit of the local taxing authority, as are some federal obligations; the difference, of course, is that the issuers of state and local bonds do not have access to the printing press. But in the last analysis, the safety of municipals rests on the local government's ability to raise funds through various levies. By that criterion, municipal bonds have an outstanding record of paying interest and principal, even in the darkest days of the Great Depression. A few towns and cities had to delay repayment, but most holders of municipal bonds survived that economic cataclysm.

Even in periods of towering interest rates, when debt instruments generally are not wise investments, municipal bonds are desirable because they are tax exempt—for different levels of government do not tax one another's revenues and securities. In addition, the original statutes establishing the federal income tax in 1913 specifically exempted municipal bonds from the federal levy. The exemption does more than give investors tax-free income: It primarily enables state and local governments to borrow money for socially and economically desirable projects at cheaper rates than private businesses. Even though the rates are generally below those of corporate borrowers, the tax-exempt yields are higher than the yields of taxable securities. The net result is that a taxpayer in a high tax bracket is better off with a low tax-free coupon than a higher taxable coupon

Over the years, the rates on municipal bonds have fluctuated dramatically. In 1946, municipal bond yields hit an all-time low of 1.29 percent; in 1982, they reached an all-time high of 13.44 percent. In recent years, there has been a three- or four-point spread between municipal bonds and corporate bonds. For the investor, the yield on a taxable investment can be fixed only after one's tax bracket has been determined. Once that is known, a comparison can be made to see which investment is better. To calculate the equivalent taxable yield for a municipal bond (around par), divide the tax-free yield by 100 percent, minus the applicable tax bracket:

$$\frac{6\% \text{ (Tax-free municipal)}}{100\% - 36\% \text{ (Tax bracket)}} = 9.38\%$$

Thus, someone in a 36 percent tax bracket would have to have a 9.38 percent taxable yield in order to have the same after-tax income as a tax-free municipal yielding 6 percent. To put it more graphically, for a husband and wife filing a joint return, the following figures show the advantage of municipals for three income levels

Taxable Income	Tax Bracket	Tax-Free Municipal 6% Bond	Taxable Corporate 8% Bond	To Keep 6% a Taxable Bond Must Pay
$36,900	28%	6%	5.76%	8.33%
89,150	31	6	5.52	8.70
140,000	36	6	5.12	9.38
250,000	39.6 6	6	4.832	9.93

Clearly, the higher the tax bracket, the more advantageous the yield of tax-free municipals compared with the after-tax return on other fixed-interest investments.

Some Municipals Are More Equal Than Others

There are half a dozen or so types of municipal bonds—all tax-free, but each with different streams of revenues: general obligation bonds, revenue bonds, special tax bonds, industrial revenue bonds, housing authority bonds and tax or revenue anticipation notes. General obligation and revenue bonds are the two principal types of municipals. General obligation bonds traditionally provide funds for capital improvements, but in the mid-1970s, revenue bonds rapidly surpassed them as a source of funds for development; they now account for two-thirds of all tax-exempt financing. General obligation bonds are backed by tax collections of the town, city or taxing authority that issues them. Consequently, everyone who pays taxes is forced to contribute to the project at hand, whether it be a sewer system or a skating rink. (On occasion, the two types have overlapped. In the 1870s, South Carolina issued $22 million of general obligation bonds, far in excess of the state's debt limit of $1.2 million, but they were to be paid off in part by the revenue of houses of ill repute. Naturally, the issues were known as "whorehouse bonds.") The tax revolts of the 1970s and early 1980s reflected taxpayer unhappiness with rising local rates—and ended with referendums, propositions and laws restricting the taxing abilities of municipalities.

In 1986 the Tax Reform Act limited the purposes for which munis could be issued tax-free for federal purposes. Some "private activities" such as pollution control bonds were denied tax-free status, while other private activity bonds were limited to strict rationing, and further subjected to an Alternative Minimum Tax (AMT). Shelters and write-offs from preference items (private activity issues underwritten after August 7, 1986) must compute their taxes in both the regular way and in the AMT fashion, adding back some of the deductions and exclusions. Taxpayers must pay whichever is greater, the regular way with deductions or 26 percent on the first $175,000 of the second way without deductions, and 28 percent of the excess.

Not many citizens are subject to the AMT (about 270,000 filers out of 113,000,000 taxpayers). Lebenthal & Co., a municipal bond firm, suggests that "the average taxpayer doesn't have enough preference income to incur the AMT liability. ... If you don't have enough preference income to trigger the AMT, if the AMT doesn't even come close to hitting home, for you AMT bonds are a windfall." Thus it may pay to shop for AMT-designated bonds.

When a general obligation bond is issued (frequently a voter referendum is required), the municipality is placing its full faith, credit and taxing power on the line. The bond ordinance or resolution is a contract between the issuer and purchaser, agreeing to the dollar amount, the coupon yield, the maturity schedule and other relevant conditions.

Revenue bonds depend not on the backing of local taxpayers but on the revenue (earnings) of the project being financed. For example, water systems, utility systems, turnpikes and port authorities all levy fees, rates or toll charges for their use. Since the projects are not backed by taxpayers, they usually do not need a general referendum for approval. Revenue bonds are a political godsend since they affect only the people using the facility. Originally a limited tool to finance public service enterprises, revenue bonds are now being used creatively to finance everything from convention centers and multifamily and low-interest housing to pollution control, resource recycling and industrial parks. The completed projects stand as security for the bondholders, and the stream of revenues are pledged to service the debt.

The other types of municipal bonds are more specific in their use: Special tax bonds are a limited form of a general obligation bond, but their issuer does not put his full faith and credit behind them—only the collected taxes of specially designated items such as alcohol, gasoline or tobacco.

Municipal bonds are long-term instruments, but some short-term municipal notes have maturities of 60 days to 1 year. These revenue or tax anticipation notes are usually issued to tide the municipality over until scheduled receipts are due. As with T-bills, these notes are sold at a discount from their face value.

Unlike federal government paper, municipals are graded by the rating agencies. Naturally, the criteria are different from those used to evaluate corporate debt: tax collection levels, property rates, levels of previous indebtedness and constitutional debt limits, economic environment and industrial prospects. The ratings are useful to investors but are perhaps more meaningful to the issuing municipality, since setting the coupon rate has a direct relationship to its rating.

Investors are sometimes leery of investing in municipal bonds because newspapers carry only abbreviated lists of market prices. Anyone wishing to monitor the bond market should read the *Daily Bond Buyer*, the trade paper for the industry. It also publishes the leading index, the *Bond Buyer Index*, an average of 20 typical bonds with 20-year maturities.

Bonds in the municipal market are usually issued in $5,000 units, so an offering price of 75 in the secondary market means that the price for a $5,000 bond is 75 percent of its face value, or $3,750. It is possible to buy a $1,000 bond from a bond dealer who specializes in odd-lot, "baby bonds," but the usual trading block is at least 5 bonds with a par value of $5,000 per bond or 20 bonds with a par value of $100,000. There are hundreds of bond dealers in the OTC market, and they will usually quote about a two-point spread between bid and ask prices in active issues, slightly larger spreads in inactive issues. For traders in bonds, the dollar price is obviously a consideration, since the profitability of the transaction will be determined by the rise and fall of bond prices as they react inversely to fluctuating interest rates. But the dollar price is nothing more than a result of the coupon rate, maturity and yield. For investors, the dollar price is not the main consideration; their primary concern is the yield to maturity. Consequently, municipals are sold on this basis—the percentage return on their money over the time the bonds are held.

Safety First

The rapid growth of the municipal market—roughly 40,000 taxing authorities—has created issues with all sorts of innovations. Because the fiscal health of many municipalities deteriorated badly during the early 1980s, some of these innovations are defensive.

One way to compete for investors' attention is to raise rates: In 1974, general obligation bonds had to pay only 77 percent of 20-year Treasury bonds. By 1993 the figure was over 90 percent of Treasury bonds. Some municipalities have purchased insurance on their bonds, which not only improves their credit ratings but helps to hold down the coupon rate. Investors feel more secure if an issue is insured with the American Municipal Bond Assurance Corporation, the Municipal Bond Insurance Association or on occasion by a commercial bank, which would redeem the bond if for some reason the state or city ran out of funds. Municipalities that purchase insurance usually guarantee themselves a AAA rating from Standard & Poor's.

Safety has been increasingly important to investors since the default in 1983 by the Washington Public Power Supply System and the decision by Washington State's highest court that the contract between the system and the 88 electric utilities to support its construction program through a take-or-pay provision was invalid. The take-or-pay clause, also known as a "hell or high water contract," secured the $2.25 billion nuclear Projects 4 and 5 bonds. The court's ruling destroyed the value of the bonds, which traded at less than 20 cents on the dollar the day after the decision and threw a monkey wrench into the financing of electric power construction in the nation.

The Orange County bankruptcy certainly stopped the muni market dead in its tracks for a brief time while the damage was assayed. But the problems were not in the basic bonds, but in the complex leveraging of derivative instruments, as noted earlier. After a reassessment, the muni market continued, more cautious about what county treasurers were doing in the name of public finance.

While most municipal issues are quite secure, the search for absolute safety continues. The latest innovation is bonds of commercial banks and savings and loan associations that are not only tax-free but guaranteed by the Federal Deposit Insurance Corporation (FDIC). The proceeds from bond sales are used to buy certificates of deposit issued by these financial institutions, which are insured by these federal insurance corporations. The banks and the savings and loan associations in turn loan their funds to finance various multi-family rental projects. The certificates of deposit mature in time to pass through and pay off the tax-exempt bonds even if the loans are in default. These FDIC-insured municipals are guaranteed, up to $100,000 per account, even though they do not have a full faith and credit backing. Again, the insurance evokes a AAA rating from Standard & Poor's.

Another way of achieving security is to put up as little money as possible to purchase financial instruments that will almost certainly appreciate in future years. Inevitably, many bond issues are at a discount in that they were originally offered with lower coupon rates than are presently obtainable. Deep discount bonds may also be the result of interest rate fluctuations or a business's running into difficulties and not paying its bondholders. While the company struggles to revamp itself or undergoes reorganization under the court's protection, the bonds will fall sharply. Buyers of such deeply discounted bonds stand to make substantial capital gains and accrued interest if or when the company emerges from its troubles. Depending on why these bonds are deeply discounted (some issues are not of investment quality), they can be particularly attractive to individuals. They yield more since they are not sought after by financial institutions, the major purchasers of bond issues. Any capital gain to an institution is taxed as ordinary income, but to individuals the maximum tax on any capital gain is only 28 percent. Moreover, deeply discounted bonds are generally available only in small lots, not in the large amounts required by institutions.

In the last few years, the corporate and municipal bond worlds have started to issue a variation on deeply discounted bonds called "original issue discount bonds." In the municipals, they are long-term bonds issued far below par value but with coupons for annual tax-free income.

There is no capital gains tax at maturity, which of course increases the yield at maturity. Another popular variation is the tax-free zero-coupon bond: There are no semiannual interest payments, but compounded interest is received when the bonds reach maturity. They are issued at very deep discounts.

Finally, the municipal market has also devised a deferred interest bond: Issued at par, the bond pays no interest until maturity; in other words, at maturity the principal and all interest accrued and compounded over the life of the bond are paid out. Because some of these variations defer the interest for 20 or 30 years, it is important to make sure the issuer is offering investment-grade paper or insurance.

Since diversity also provides security, a number of municipal bond funds have sprung up to further reduce the risk for investors. The plain vanilla of municipal funds is the unit investment trust, a closed-end fund (a pool of limited dollars) with a fixed portfolio of different municipal bonds. Interest is paid regularly, and upon maturity the principal is distributed. Since these unit trusts do not change their portfolios, problem issues must be held by the trust and absorbed by the trust investor. However, there is a secondary market for such trust units.

The other municipal fund possibility is the open-ended mutual fund (an unlimited pool of dollars that increases or decreases depending on sales and redemptions of fund shares) with a changeable portfolio. Shares of tax-exempt funds are quoted daily in the press and the funds will repurchase an investor's shares. Unit trusts are more popular since they are sold more aggressively, even though they have a sales charge and the mutual funds usually do not. However, the unseen advisory fees are higher with the funds than they are with the trusts.

CHAPTER 4

The Federal Reserve System

The way to make sure of power and influence is by lending money confidentially to your neighbors at a small interest, or perhaps no interest at all, and having their bonds in your possession.

—Boswell's *Life of Dr. Johnson*

Tools of the Trade

The year 1913 was not memorable in American history, but it saw the creation of two fundamental financial institutions: the personal income tax and the Federal Reserve System. Today, there is no escaping the impact that taxes and Federal Reserve policies have on economic life.

The Federal Reserve System is the nation's central bank. As an autonomous organization, it is charged by Congress with maintaining the monetary stability of the nation's economy. Naturally, its actions, its lack of actions and its perceived actions have an enormous impact on financial markets. The impact is derived from the Fed's role in five distinct activities: (1) balancing the supply of money and credit in circulation; (2) regulating and supervising the nation's banking system; (3) creating money and providing clearance facilities for checks; (4) serving as the government's fiscal agent; and (5) serving as the agent for foreign central banks. Actions taken in any of these areas are subject to intense scrutiny by the financial world.

The Fed now publishes information that was once zealously guarded. Indeed, for decades the actions of the Fed were rarely questioned. When a reporter asked a pointed question of Benjamin Strong, the head of the System in the 1920s, he replied, "That, sir, is none of your business." That kind of response no longer washes. The Congress, users of the Freedom of Information Act, the White House, the financial community and the media all cajole and threaten the Fed to explain what it is doing when it "targets" the money supply, "tightens" credit, "lowers" interest rates, "opens" the discount window or "swaps" a foreign currency.

While the Fed's behavior has always been of concern to business, it was not until the mid-1970s that an aroused Congress demanded greater accountability—in brief, to know what policies the central bank was pursuing. A compromise was arrived at: Twice a year the Fed reports to Congress on its targets for monetary growth. Since there is a direct correlation between the quantity of money and an expanding economy, it is important for the central bank to ascertain the right targets, or credit conditions, for optimal growth.

For the next few years, the Fed used a variety of tools to hit its monetary targets, with only fair success. Meanwhile, inflation accelerated and the value of the dollar dwindled.

The monetary tools the Fed uses remain the same, but the mix and emphasis are forever changing as new economic doctrines become fashionable. The system uses three primary techniques to govern the economy: (1) the discount rate; (2) reserve requirements; and (3) open market operations. Which tool it employs is a function of the Fed's viewpoint and the policy it wishes to pursue.

The discount rate is the interest rate the central bank charges its member banks when they borrow at the discount window. Not all banks are members of the Federal Reserve System, but a majority are, especially the major or money center banks. When these banks are strapped for reserves, they can borrow at the Fed; sometimes the discount rate is cheaper than money market rates. This is a bit ironic, since the discount rate was originally conceived as a penalty rate to be imposed on banks that lent too liberally or injudiciously.

Banks can use other means to cover a deficiency in their legal reserves. They can borrow Federal funds (overnight monies from other banks), draw down balances with other banks, borrow Eurodollars, issue certificates of deposit or sell money market assets like government securities. It is up to the individual bank to make that judgment based on costs and other advantages. But only borrowing from the Fed's discount window increases the money supply; all the other methods simply redistribute reserves from one bank to another. And borrowing from the Fed prevents a shortage of reserves from spreading to other banks and shrinking the money supply unintentionally.

Consequently, the central bank can purposely increase or decrease the money supply by lowering or raising the discount rate it charges member banks. The discount rate is a special signal to the money markets, an indication of which way the Fed would like interest rates to move.

This was the case in the late 1980s and early 1990s when there was a crisis of confidence in the savings and loan industry and the banking system. Money center banks were perceived to be going out of business, and share prices fell to unimaginable lows. The Fed stepped in and flooded the system with liquidity. In turn the banks were able to borrow at the discount window at extraordinarily cheap rates—3 percent—only to turn around and buy U.S. government securities that were yielding 6 percent more. (A twist on the old observation that bankers live by the 3-6-3 rule: borrow at 3 percent, lend at 6 percent and be out of the shop by three o'clock.

The second instrument in the Fed's arsenal is the reserve requirement imposed on member banks. Each member bank is required to maintain a fixed percentage of its deposits with the central bank as a guarantee of its liquidity. In recent years reserve requirements have been in the 10 percent to 18 percent range. (The reserve requirements differ for time deposits and demand deposits.) Reserves have a direct bearing on the credit a bank can extend in the form of loans, investments and deposits. The smaller the amount of reserves required, the greater the amount of potential credit expansion. Reserve requirements do not make a bank more liquid; they merely control the amount of credit and, in turn, the money supply.

The Fed is concerned with the excess reserves, the amount above what is required. If the central bank finds that these excess reserves are too little, and are therefore not providing the Reserve System with enough lendable funds, the Fed may cut the discount rate or buy government securities in the open market to inject more money into the system. Of course, the same result would be achieved if the reserve requirements were lowered. However, the Fed adjusts reserve requirements relatively infrequently. Conversely, the central bank can reduce the amount of excess or free reserves by raising reserve requirements, by raising the discount rate and/or by selling government securities to take money out of circulation.

Bank reserves are carefully watched since they are, in a sense, high-powered money: Due to a multiplier effect, a small percentage change in reserves can make a significant change in the money supply. This is perhaps most clearly seen in the third major tool of the Fed, the open market operations of the Open Market Committee. This committee lays down guidelines for the buying and selling of government securities, a function only the Fed, not the Treasury, is allowed to undertake. Technically, only the Fed can create money out of thin air by writing a check for the purchase of government securities.

The purchase of $500 million worth of Treasury paper will put that amount of funds into the commercial banks of the dealers in government securities. These commercial banks will place the required amount in their reserves—say 15 percent of the amount they receive—and lend out the other 85 percent. This chain of events will spread to the second, third and other levels of lending. Eventually, the multiplier effect will increase the original half-billion dollars approximately six times, a total of $3 billion. Thus, the Fed has increased the money supply through open market operations by buying government bonds from banks, insurance companies, pension funds and other financial institutions.

Open market operations have an immediate and profound impact on bank reserves and the money supply. They also affect an equally important factor: interest rates. Fed buying or selling can have a direct influence on short-term rates, and the increase or decrease in reserves can affect the Federal funds rate, the monies banks lend to each other on a daily basis to cover their reserve positions.

With all these options at its disposal, the Fed has never been able to work with great precision since our society is so large, diverse and complex. Any attempt to move the economy in a particular direction is fraught with statistical and political pitfalls.

The Monies Supplied

However, adjustments to the discount rate or required reserves and open market operations are carried out with but one of two goals: to accelerate economic growth or to retard it. If the economy is expanding too quickly and developing strong inflationary tendencies, the Fed steps in to reduce the amount of money in circulation, or at least reduce the rate of growth while it attempts to raise interest rates. Conversely, if the economy is in a recession, it takes steps to increase the money supply and make credit more readily available through lower interest rates. In its most active phases, the Fed constantly appears to be leaning against the wind.

The Fed's job is made particularly frustrating by the economy's apparent unwillingness to respond to the central bank's poking and prodding. Moreover, the central bank has in the immediate past changed strategies and tactics. At one time it was most concerned with the level of interest rates; at another, with the growth of the money supply. And for all its recent openness, the Fed still speaks with a forked tongue or a bureaucratese that seems to cloud its objectives purposely.

For a number of years after it started to announce its monetary targets publicly, the central bank's lack of determination, contradictory fiscal policies and lack of political leadership caused the value of the dollar to depreciate rapidly in world markets. Finally, in October 1979, the Fed announced that it would no longer pay such close attention to the level of interest rates but be more concerned with the money supply. Faced with rapidly accelerating inflation, it adopted an increasingly popular view of monetarist economists—that it could most effectively control inflation by regulating the level of bank reserves.

For the next three years, money aggregates, or simply the money supply, became the thing to watch; in fact, the money supply became an object of cult veneration by the financial world as it attempted to divine the Fed's meaning every Thursday afternoon at 4:15 PM, when the figures were released.

Upon the release of these figures, there will be an immediate reaction in the OTC bond market, which is still open for trading. If the figures exceed the presumed targets, reflecting a surge of money with its inflationary overtones, there is likely to be a selloff: a decline in bond prices and consequent rise in yields. Conversely, if the aggregates are below expectation, this may well be interpreted in a positive way: a rise in bond prices and a lowering of yields. The reaction of the markets is never the same, for much depends on what is expected on a weekly basis. And since the same monetary skirmish is never fought twice, the results are forever surprising.

The other markets—stock, commodity and foreign exchange—will also react to the previous day's figures when they open.

The day after the Fed releases its figures, the press carries a synopsis with the most significant figures in bold type:

FEDERAL RESERVE

Money Aggregates (Average in billions of dollars.)

	One year ended		Annual growth rates		
	Feb 27	Feb 20	3 mos.	6 mos.	12 mos.
M-1	1,145.9	1,145.4	−0.3%	−0.3%	1.4%
M-2	3,622.6	3,620.7	1.3	0.5	1.9
M-3	4,348.0	4,333.5	3.5	2.5	1.9

The money supply has a number of definitions. The most common one is M1, which measures immediate transaction money, or money in cash and checking accounts. M2 includes M1 plus somewhat less liquid transaction money: money market mutual funds, savings accounts and some time deposits. M3 includes the two previous Ms plus even less liquid assets, such as short-term bonds, Treasury securities and commercial paper. The M1 is most closely watched, for it provides an immediate clue to the actions of the Fed and credit conditions.

From October 1979 to October 1982, the Fed, fearful of runaway inflation, manipulated the money aggregates. This great experiment in monetarism brought about towering interest rates as it reduced the growth rate of money, but it also precipitated the most severe recession since the Great Depression. All the blame should not be laid at the feet of the Federal Reserve System, for administration policy, as manifested in the 1981 tax act, provided a great deal of fiscal stimulus by enacting three years of substantial tax cuts. With monetary and fiscal policies at loggerheads, the country drifted deeper into recession.

By October 1982, the combination of a prolonged domestic recession, a weakness in foreign economies, double-digit unemployment and budget deficits rapidly reaching the $200 billion mark had prompted the Fed to switch its emphasis. Even though the money supply has a direct, if belated, influence on economic growth, it had become increasingly difficult over those years to spell out what the money supply really encompassed.

Part of the problem stemmed from the original attempt to define the money supply; the Fed measures transaction balances or monies rather than money used as savings or a storehouse of value. The basic presumption is that there is a stable and consistent relationship between the amount of money that businesses and people wish to hold and the total of dollar transactions in the economy. Thus, the presumption continues that the amount of credit can be controlled (through the Fed's intervention) by anticipating the public's holdings or demands for money.

What knocked these presumptions into a cocked hat is the fundamental assumption that targets for the money supply could be based on the psychological considerations of the public, whether to hold more or less money. But what further undermined the process was the changing nature of transaction money. With all sorts of new money instruments (such as money market funds) to circumvent monetary controls (such as Fed regulations that limited bank interest rates) and to escape from the inflationary bind, people blurred the distinction between savings and cash, investments and instant liquidity. The public ran their balances up and down for new reasons, reasons not anticipated by the Fed. As a result, the Fed's targets were missed by significant margins.

The Fed has decided that watching the narrow monetary aggregates was illusory and not as productive as watching the whole economy—unemployment and employment rates, plant capacity, real income, productivity, trade balances and consumer prices. This shift marked yet another turning point in its history of monetary control. Nevertheless, a whole generation of "Fed watchers" continues to assay, evaluate and analyze the weekly publication of money supply figures as a clue to the direction of monetary policy. However, instead of watching the narrower monetary aggregate, M1, the present tendency is to watch M2, a broader gauge with more substantial predictive powers. Moreover, it is the one monetary figure used by the Department of Commerce in its index of leading economic indicators.

Finally, in 1993, the chairman of the Federal Reserve System, Alan Greenspan, switched the Fed's emphasis once more, since monetary aggregates seemed neither productive nor prophetic. Henceforth, the Fed would pay more attention to interest rates, as it had before October 1979.

In early 1994 the Fed moved aggressively to shut down the flow of liquidity it had unleashed three years earlier to counter the banking scare. Fearing a growing threat of inflation, the Fed raised the federal funds rate and the discount rate seven times from February 1994 through January 1995.

The Fed chairman's subsequent Congressional testimony suggested that not only interest rates were being closely monitored, but all commodities—and especially the price of gold. Inflation never did appear in any virulent form, but the Fed would no doubt stress that its actions defeated it before it had a chance to appear.

A Matter of Inflation

This massive concentration by the capital markets on the money supply is essentially a national concern over inflation. Since the end of the Vietnam War, inflation has severely eroded the purchasing power of earnings and savings. Every recent administration has termed inflation the nation's No. 1 economic problem. While economists debate its causes, most concede that a rapidly expanding money supply, along with enormous budget deficits, almost always precedes an inflationary period.

So while the government and the Fed have officially fought inflation, the public has been split. In the 1970s, a large segment of society found inflation not only tolerable but welcome. They made up the hard core of the inflationary constituency. Those who profited by inflation were wage earners and salaried personnel, who had their pay tied to cost-of-living allowances, and Social Security recipients and pensioners, who received benefit adjustments. Frequently, the pay and benefits were adjusted by the consumer price index or some other index that generously overcompensated for actual price increases.

Inflation had some benefit for savers, too, as high money market rates, which became available to the public through money market funds and deregulation of bank accounts, provided substantial increases in interest income. The search for higher interest reached epidemic proportions as billions of dollars were "disintermediated"—savings were removed from low-interest accounts to be deposited in high-interest accounts.

Finally, even in the face of towering interest rates, members of this inflationary constituency realized that in real terms, interest rates were low due to the very nature of our tax system. Since interest charges were deductible from both personal and corporate tax returns, what at first appeared to be a formidable rate was actually nominal to borrowers. The 1986 tax reforms changed all that by disallowing interest charges for personal debt, except for investments and home mortgages.

Lenders, on the other hand, are penalized by the tax system in a period of inflation. Since a lender must pay taxes on his total or nominal interest earnings, not the real or depreciated earnings, he is being overtaxed on his interest income. Indeed, in the 1970s, according to one Fed study, a lender's real after-tax yield averaged close to zero.

When the rate of inflation subsided in 1982 and 1983, interest rates, paradoxically, began to inflict real pain. With the prime rate still in the double-digit range of 12 percent, the consumer price index receded to less than half that, about 4 percent. Even though nominal interest rates are considerably lower than before, real interest rates of 8 percent are harder to live with. It was not very long ago that 3 percent was considered "normal." Consequently, the capital markets are extremely sensitive to the money supply. On the one hand, massive government deficits appear to be a permanent part of the financial landscape, requiring large government borrowings that will inevitably cause upward pressure on interest rates. On the other hand, if the money supply is not increased, government borrowings will crowd out private sector borrowing, aborting a recovery or reducing the expansive phase of the business cycle.

And lurking in the background is the threat of more inflation. If the Fed is too accommodating, inflation is likely to follow even if the first results are lower interest rates. If the Fed is not accommodating enough, recession may follow even if the first consequences are higher interest rates. Within this web of seeming contradiction, the success of the Fed's role as master manipulator rests on its ability to adjust or tune the money supply and interest rates in consonance with the economy.

The split constituencies, borrowers and lenders, showed their special interests in the early 1990s. With inflation under control and the Fed opening the floodgates of liquidity, interest rates dropped. Indeed at the start of 1994, banks were offering 2 percent or less on CDs. Borrowers were of course immensely pleased. But the cries from the lenders, many of whom augmented their incomes from high yields, were deafening. Clearly the tensions between rentiers and debtors is an eternal one. And the Fed is caught in the balancing act.

In passing, it should be noted that the major fear of inflation derives from the huge deficits (from both the current trade account and the federal budget) to which the U.S. has been prone for a decade and a half. Towering debt structure, the Fed reasoned, would guarantee inflation, which in turn would return bond yields and the prime rates of banks to the astronomic levels of the late 1970s and early 1980s. Yet the worry seems misplaced. Looking back at the last decade or so, James Grant, publisher of the astute *Grant's Interest Rate Observer*, noted in early 1995: "The public debt has grown from a trillion dollars when the long bond yield was 15 percent to more than four trillion, and now the long bond yields 7¾ percent. I think there are a lot of reasons to favor fiscal rectitude, but I don't think those reasons realistically concern the level of bond yields."

In brief, it just may be a great misconception or simplification to correlate inflation with widening deficits, resulting in dramatically higher interest rates. Another misunderstanding, also fostered by the Fed and the U.S. Treasury, was the notion that a form of benign neglect with regard to the U.S. dollar would be beneficial. Even worse was the actual active intervention to depress the dollar's value in the foreign exchange markets. This would boost exports and diminish the large trade deficits, especially with Japan. The government undertook the curious policy of trashing its own currency.

The Palace Accords in September 1985, precipitated by U.S. Treasury Secretary James Baker, was aimed at precisely that goal. For the next decade, under Republican and Democratic presidents, the dollar was *persona non grata* in its own home. The $35 billion trade deficit with Japan, however, was not cured; rather it nearly doubled by 1995, even though the value of the yen moved from 240 to 86 to the dollar. Similar revaluations took place with European currencies. Thus the Fed and Treasury action dramatically depressed the value of their unit of account in the quest for some ephemeral goal, redounding to the loss of purchasing power for their own greenback.

Is there a moral to government monetary action in the last decade with regard to inflation? For investors there was a double whammy: a depressed dollar and a surge of money creation after 1990 when the Fed ballooned the monetary base by 35 percent over the next four years. Only the deflation of the early 1990s, with its reduced demand for credit, prevented a bout of serious inflation. Only when it became apparent that inflation might be the consequence did the Fed clamp down on interest rates by raising short-term rates seven times in one year, 1994–95. That year was indeed a devastating one for investors in fixed-income securities—reportedly the worst market performance in the bond market since 1927. It is not unreasonable to suggest that governments create inflationary conditions, then do more damage when they move to control (read *correct*) their previous malpractices.

Who Sets Interest Rates?

In an open economy, no one group—consumers, banks, labor, management or even the majestic federal government—is sufficiently powerful to set interest rates, but the Fed does have more direct influence on rates than any other institution. The behavior of the Federal Reserve System is closely watched by the financial world, for its actions have both an immediate impact and long-term consequences.

Although the Fed does not dictate the level of rates, its activities can, certainly, prod the rates in one direction or the other. When the Fed adopts a restrictive policy that will push rates higher by means of open market operations, the discount rate and bank reserves, the monetary aggregates fall. Thus a series of clear signals are sent: that inflation will be fought, a too-expansive economy cooled, and the "long green" that makes the equity markets go will be in shorter supply. And the opposite of this tightening, monetary ease, sends its own special signals: A little inflation may not be a bad thing, underutilized capacity needs stimulating and the investment scene needs a boost to increase capital formation.

Perhaps the most sensitive interest signals are the federal funds and the prime rate, the rate at which commercial banks lend to their most creditworthy customers. While these rates are most visible and widely commented upon, they simply reflect the Fed's stance of ease or tightness. Various stratagems have been developed over the years to help market participants in their quest for that ultimate signal. An old cliché in the marketplace is that no one rings a bell when it's time to buy or sell. Still, the search goes on, and some observers use the Fed as the ultimate bell ringer.

The weekly money supply figures offer what is obviously a very short-term measurement, whereas an adjustment in bank reserves is a long-term indicator. If reserve requirements are reduced, the action foretells a rise in stock prices over the next 12 to 18 months. An increase in those reserve requirements foretells a decline in stock prices. While this indicator has reasonable prophetic accuracy, it doesn't come into play very often, for the Fed adjusts reserve requirements only once every two or three years.

A more immediate signal is the change in the discount rate, which is manipulated often and frequently: In the last six months of 1982, the discount rate was lowered eight times. It was this lowering, and anticipated lowering, that set the stage and roused the equity market to advance explosively for the next year. And as we have seen, the Fed raised a combination of the discount rate and the federal fund rate seven times within 12 months in 1994–95. In turn, prices in the fixed-income markets plummeted as yields rose.

KEY INTEREST RATES
(published daily or weekly in the financial press)

- Discount Rate
- Prime Rate
- Federal Funds (day-to-day money)
- Treasury Bills (91 days)
- Government Bonds (long-term)
- Commercial Paper (3 months)
- Corporate/Industrial Bonds
- Municipal Bonds
- Bank Time Deposits (Certificates of Deposit)
- Eurocurrencies

The Fed and the Market

The Fed is also charged with controlling credit within the stock markets. It does this by setting margin requirements, the amount a customer can borrow from a broker to finance dealings. The interest rate the brokerage house charges the investor for a debit balance is not regulated by the Fed but is based on market considerations. Since 1974, the margin requirement has remained steady at 50 percent. In addition to the Fed's rule, brokerage firms are obliged to enforce the maintenance requirement set by the New York Stock Exchange. The regulation stipulated that a customer's equity (less the broker's loan) should be no less than 25 percent of the market value of the securities in the margin account. Should they fall below that value, a margin call is sent out asking for more collateral. If the investor cannot come up with the required amount of cash (or securities whose value equals that amount), then the broker sells stock from the investor's account

Specifically, a margin account can borrow up to half (with the margin rate at 50 percent) the value of a purchase. For instance, in order to buy 200 shares at $50, or $10,000 worth of stock, the customer puts up $5,000, and the remaining $5,000 is lent by the broker, usually at one or two percentage points above the broker's discount rate (the rate at which brokers borrow from banks). While listed securities may be hypothecated (that is, pledged as collateral for a loan), only some over-the-counter issues are so designated by the Fed. Should the stock appreciate to $75 a share and the investor sell, the $15,000 would net a gain of $5,000, less interest charges for the loan and brokerage commissions. The leverage of borrowing has enabled the customer to gain 100 percent on the funds instead of the 50 percent gained by purchasing the shares outright.

But leverage is a two-way street. If the value of the purchase falls from $10,000 to $6,600 ($33 per share), after deducting the broker's $5,000 loan, the client would be left with only $1,600. At this point the investor would receive a margin call, since the maintenance requirement insists that equity should exceed 25 percent of the shares' market value (25 percent of $6,600 equals $1,650). The borrower then has three options: to sell out the position and take a loss; to put up enough cash to restore the margin account; or to deliver enough collateral in the form of additional shares to meet the maintenance requirement.

Margin requirements are important credit checks for the Fed. Today, only 10 percent of the investing public maintains margin accounts—quite a contrast to 1929, when 40 percent of stockholders were operating on margin. Moreover, in the twenties it was possible—indeed, it was the practice—to buy stock on 10 percent or 20 percent cash and to borrow the rest. This technique led to a form of pyramiding, borrowing additional funds for further purchases on the basis of paper profits. The leverage was so great that many economists point to it as being solely responsible for the Crash. Since then, the Fed has kept a tight rein on margin trading.

CHAPTER 5

Options

*Take calculated risks. That is quite different
from being rash.*

—George S. Patton

Conservation versus Speculation

Options have been around as long as capitalism, perhaps longer. But in the eminent words of an early edition of the *Encyclopaedia Britannica*, there are "few men in London, usually foreigners, who have the reputation of being exceptionally clever in this class of dealing, and of making large profits out of it."

This cautionary note remains true: Today, there are still few men and women who make large profits, but whereas the options market was once for professionals only, it is now peopled with amateurs as well. Until 1973, options on stocks had to be purchased through put and call brokers, over-the-counter dealers who specialized in matching buyers and sellers. But then a revolution took hold in the marketplace; options began to be listed and traded on the new Chicago Board of Options Exchange (CBOE) and then on other exchanges across the country. With this listing and the establishment of a central clearing corporation (Options Clearing Corporation), which acts as a participant and guarantor on the other side of the transaction, stock options became respectable and volume in them virtually exploded.

An option is a contract that gives the purchaser the right to buy an asset from the seller for a fixed price during a fixed period of time. The assets can be any number of things— land, houses, agricultural commodities or film rights to a novel—but in this instance the underlying asset is common stock in a round lot, 100 shares per contract.

In securities markets there are two kinds of options—a call and a put. A call gives the purchaser the right to buy the asset, whereas a put gives the buyer the right to put or place the asset with the seller. On the other side of both transactions is the seller, known as the option writer. In the call, the writer, for an agreed price, guarantees to produce the asset when the buyer decides to execute his right to purchase. In the case of a put, the writer agrees, again for a price, to accept the asset.

From these simple definitions arise a wide variety of combinations. But it must be emphasized that an option is a choice: The buyer pays for the privilege of executing or not executing his contract. The obligation exists only on the other side of the contract: The person collecting the money is guaranteeing fulfillment when the buyer chooses to consummate. In brief, an option is a one-way arrangement.

Listed options have become popular for a number of reasons.

- They are cheaper to buy than the underlying securities.
- They have an active secondary market so they can easily be traded.
- They are highly visible due to their daily listing in the financial pages.
- They provide leverage to increase profits as well as losses.
- They limit risk.
- They enable an investor to acquire a position before his cash flow could cover the full investment.
- They can be used as another investment device to diversify a portfolio.

Before analyzing the mechanics of option trading, we should discuss the purposes options serve. As with most things financial, there are two schools of thought. On the one hand, it is widely perceived by the public that options are speculative instruments. Indeed, many investors view them purely as gambling devices that serve no economic purpose. On the other hand, no less than a Nobel laureate has provided economic justification for the use of options. Even the federal government has lent economic legitimacy to options by giving them favorable tax consideration.

The split in opinion is more than academic. Money managers entrusted with other people's money face a dilemma as to whether or not it is prudent to use options. Fiduciaries certainly cannot assume the license to speculate. But if low-risk options offer an opportunity to improve the rate of return on their supervised funds, then perhaps prudence dictates their use. It is an open question, since options can be used both to speculate and to conserve.

Call Options

The most popular option is a call option. No doubt its popularity arises from the same bias that the investing public exhibits in the market: Most investors buy securities (buy long) in the hope that they will appreciate, rather than sell them (sell short) on the assumption that they will depreciate. Perhaps it is just human nature to be optimistic, for experience shows that while prices do indeed have an upward tilt, prices fall almost as frequently as they rise.

Listed call options are carried in the financial pages, next to the stock tables. Each major exchange lists its options by class, including all the options of the underlying security. Thus, a company will have listed below it the daily closing price of the underlying stock and all the strike prices of the various options. The strike price is the price at which the call buyer will purchase the shares should he decide to exercise his option. These prices will vary, depending on investor interest and the volatility of the shares; in the case of well-known companies, there may be more than half a dozen prices listed. The market prices for options may change every day, but options with new strike prices are established only when prices of the underlying shares have moved significantly. Purchasers usually have a choice of several striking prices, established at $5 or $10 intervals. For stocks selling below $50 a share, the intervals are $5 above and below the stock's price; for those selling above $50, they are $10.

To the right of each strike price are the premiums, the price per share for an option of 100 shares. The first three columns are for calls, the last three for puts. At any given time, a buyer or seller of options has a choice of three expiration dates, three months apart from each other. A listed option can be purchased right up to a few days before it expires, and the longest option runs only for nine months, expiring on the Saturday following the third Friday of the month named in the contract. When one period expires, a new period starts; each column in the financial page listing represents one expiration period. A recent innovation for some stocks and indexes is LEAPS, long-term options extending their duration for two or three years. But thus far, LEAPS are a distinct minority (for more information, see page 78).

CHICAGO BOARD OPTIONS EXCHANGE

Option/	*Strike*	*Calls-Last*			*Puts-Last*		
NYSE cl.	*Price*	*Feb*	*May*	*Aug*	*Feb*	*May*	*Aug*
Boeing	40	6⅜	7⅜	7⅝	1–16	9–16	11–16
46⅛	45	1 15–16	3¾	5⅜	3/4	2 1–16	2¾
46⅛	50	5–16	1⅝	3	4⅛	4½	r

(r—not traded)

An investor's two main concerns are whether the option is in-the-money or out-of-the-money and the expiration date. A call option that is in-the-money is one that, if exercised, will obtain the underlying shares for a price below the current market price. The option therefore has an intrinsic cash value. If the shares are selling at $50 and the option is at $42.50, the option has an intrinsic value of $7.50. If the exercise price or striking price is about the same as the market price, the option is at-the-money. And finally, a call whose striking price is above the current market price of the stock is said to be out-of-the-money.

The investor's second immediate concern is the length of life of the expiring option. An option, unlike the underlying shares, is a wasting asset and becomes less valuable with each passing day as its time value shrinks. Thus the premium for an option that is out-of-the-money will vanish as the time runs out.

Other factors affect the price of options besides being in- or out-of-the-money and the duration of the contract, but the effects of these are harder to determine.

Towering interest rates, such as those the nation has experienced in the not-too-distant past, increase the value of options since they tie up less money. One of the attractions of options is their ability not only to control more stock with less money, but to net a profit many times exceeding the profit potential of the underlying shares. When money costs less—in other words, when interest rates are low—options are somewhat less desirable.

Another influence is the demand for underlying shares. If the stock is an active and volatile one, option activity can be correspondingly hectic and option premiums will rise. The reverse is also true: Regardless of the outlook for the security, a lack of investor interest tends to reduce option premiums.

In practice, the call buyer enters the market to take advantage of the expected quick appreciation of the underlying shares. Let's say he or she purchases a six-month, at-the-money Widget Works September $40 call option in April for a premium of $4, spending a total of $400 for 100 shares. Within three months, the underlying shares of Widget Works move to $44 and the premium moves to $6, At that point, the option owner can sell the $4 option for $6, a gain of 50 percent. If he or she had purchased the shares outright, the move from $40 to $44 would have gained only a 10 percent profit. If he or she exercises the option, the profit made by buying the shares and then selling them will be cut nearly in half due to the commissions. Obviously, selling the option itself is the most lucrative action.

This example also clarifies intrinsic and time values. At the start of the six-month option period, the at-the-money option had $4 worth of time value and no intrinsic value. After three months and the subsequent rise in price, the $6 option had $4 worth of intrinsic value and $2 worth of time value. By the expiration date in September, the option will have only intrinsic value and no time value. Once the option is in-the-money, it tends to move more or less in tandem with the stock.

Had the Widget Works option moved against the buyer and fallen in three months to $36, the value of the option would have fallen to $1. If the trend continued to $30, at the end of six months the option would expire worthless. The option buyer would have lost $4 a share, or $400, but the owner of the stock itself would have lost $10 a share, or a total of $1,000. The option quickly lost its intrinsic value, then slowly lost its time value as it expired. An option that is out-of-the-money has no intrinsic value, only time value. Such options are usually very inexpensive since their likelihood of moving into-the-money is small.

Calls can also be used to protect short sales. (Short selling is the sale of stock, either shares that one owns or shares that are borrowed by a broker for that purpose. The sellers expect the shares to decline in price so they can replace them later at a profit.) Presume a short sale of Widget Works shares at $40. For a $4 ($400) premium, the investors have bought an at-the-money security blanket for six months. Should the price move against them and climb to $50, they can deliver $40 shares. The most they stand to lose is the option premium plus transaction costs. Should the shares tumble to $30, the premium would reduce their gain since the first four points would pay for the option; in this case, the short sale only becomes profitable below $36. An in-the-money call is more expensive but gives a short sale greater upside protection, while an out-of-the-money call is less expensive but affords less protection against loss if the shares advance.

Put Options

The purchaser of a put option is assuming that prices will be lower three, six or nine months later. The buyer is entitled to sell, or put, to the option writer a specified amount of stock at an agreed-upon price at any time during the length of the option. In most respects, the put is the opposite of the call option.

Put options appeal to that relatively small universe of investors who believe that prices are about to head south. This is a belief held by short sellers, regardless of economic climate and regardless of bull or bear market. For perspective, one must remember that only between 1 percent and 5 percent of the transactions on the exchanges are short sales. Short selling is not a popular pastime.

An investor who assumes that the price of an underlying stock is bound to go lower purchases a put option for one of two reasons: to safeguard a paper profit he already has or to take advantage of the decline even though he does not own that security. Both steps can be accomplished in other ways, too. If the investor owns shares, he can place a stop order, which automatically sells the shares if the price falls below a specified limit. Or he can sell the shares short if he does not actually own them, or short them against the box (so called because of the safe deposit box in which the shares he already owns are kept).

Both procedures have their own special limitations. Stop orders sometimes get executed due to minor fluctuations even though the underlying trend upward is still intact, and uncovered short sales leave an open-ended liability if the market moves up. A covered short sale (the sale of securities that are already owned) ends the liability but also terminates the holding period for tax purposes; it may give the holder a short-term gain when he planned on a long-term one.

Put options are found to the right of the call options on the listed tables. Put options are at-the-money when the underlying shares are trading at the same price as the striking price, in-the-money when options trade for less than the striking price, and out-of-the-money when they trade for more than the striking price. And, as with call options, the premiums reflect the intrinsic value as well as the time value of the options.

Here is an example of a typical put option in action. An investor owns 100 shares of Widget Works outright, or long, purchased originally for $25 each. She has become increasingly nervous about their profits and prospects. The shares are now trading for $40. Hoping to secure her profit, she turns to the financial pages, where she finds a six-month at-the-money put selling for $4, or $400 per contract. She purchases the option and within the next three months her worries are confirmed—the shares fall to $34. The price of the put rises to $10 ($1,000). The investor can pursue one of two courses of action: She can exercise the option, ridding herself of her shares for $4,000, or sell the option.

Should she choose to exercise the option, she can expect a $1,500 profit on the sale of the stock to the option writer, less the $400 premium she originally paid for the option—a profit of $1,100 (less commissions). Or she can sell the option at a profit of $600, and sell the shares for $34 at a profit of $900—a total gain of $1,500.

Whether they be calls or puts, options are highly leveraged instruments. The dramatic leverage becomes apparent if you compare a put option with a short sale. In selling shares of Widget Works short at $40, a decline in price to $35 over the next three months would provide a gain of $500—a profit of 12.5 percent. Even if the account was fully margined (at 50 percent), so that only $2,000 was needed, the profit would rise to 25 percent. On the other hand, the purchase of a six-month option for $3 ($300) would have appreciated to about $5.50 in the three months the stock declined to $35—a profit of $2.50 (or $250) if the option was sold. The profit on the original cost is 83 percent.

If the stock had not declined, the put buyer would have lost 100 percent of her capital, and her return on her investment would have been zero. In the same circumstances, the short seller would also have had a zero return on her investment but would still have had her capital. Had the price of the stock risen, the option buyer would have lost her original investment since she could not be expected to exercise, but the short seller would lose more with each point the stock advanced until she closed out the short sale.

Buyers of put and call options have three choices open to them: let the option expire, sell the option or exercise the option.

One would make the first choice if the option is near its expiration date, and therefore has no time value, and is out-of-the-money (so that it has no intrinsic value either).

The second choice—selling the option in the option market—if not profitable at least reduces the loss.

If your option is in-the-money, you might decide to exercise it. Although it is generally more profitable to sell the option and profit from its appreciation, rather than buy and sell the underlying stock (due to transaction commissions), the option buyer may wish to exercise in order to hold the shares in her portfolio.

Only 4 percent or 5 percent of all call options purchased are actually exercised. Close to 70 percent are liquidated or sold, and the remaining 25 percent simply expire. More than 80 percent of all puts are liquidated, nearly 15 percent expire, and about 5 percent are exercised.

While most options are short-term vehicles, a new form has evolved for long-term investors. The Long-term Equity AnticiPation Securities (LEAPS) are structured to provide the owner the right to purchase or sell shares of a stock at a specified price on or before a given date up to three years in the future. These LEAPS are exchange-traded puts and calls, and may be exercised on any business day prior to expiration (American style). LEAPS give investors a long-term perspective, since they do not require monitoring positions on a daily basis. Purchasers of LEAPS puts can provide a hedge against substantial declines in their own positions.

Trading Naked

It is one of the better-kept secrets in the financial world that the way to profit in the options market is not to buy puts and calls but to sell them—to be the writer rather than the purchaser. This is what financial institutions do. Option writing earns them additional returns on their portfolios, injects a note of predictability, and certifies that they are being exceedingly prudent with other people's money by protecting those funds from sudden or unwelcome price movements.

The secret, of course, is not based on guessing wrong—being bullish when you should have been bearish or vice versa—but on the simple fact that within the limited option periods of three, six, or nine months, the underlying shares do not move dramatically. This lack of motion naturally works to the advantage of the contract writer.

Most options are written against shares that are already owned. This is in contrast to uncovered, or naked, options, which are sold by an option writer who does not actually own the underlying stock. If a naked option is exercised, then the option writer must enter the market and buy the stock, at the going price, in order to sell it, at the striking price, to the call owner.

Brokerage houses require the writer of naked options to have sufficient shares or cash in his or her account to meet the terms of the contract should the call owner decide to exercise his or her option.

The difference between naked and covered option writing should be kept in mind. Covered call writers gain the price of the premiums but lose any opportunity to make a profit on their underlying shares when they exceed the striking price. Indeed, they may lose even more should they repurchase the option at a higher price. In return for the premium, they have lost the potential gain—the reason they originally established their long position. On the down side, the premium acts as a pillow, reducing their loss by the price of the contract. The net result of covered call writing is reduction of the variability of return from the portfolio. In brief, the covered call reduces risk against loss, but it also reduces the potential for significant capital appreciation.

The real question about covered call writing is: Does the premium compensate for the lost opportunity? One authority believes not: "Covered call writing is more likely to reduce portfolio returns than it is to increase them."

The option writer's profits are limited to the price of the contract, while the potential losses can be significant.

To put it somewhat differently, option writers know how much can be made from the sale of an option, but have no way of determining how much might be lost. Option buyers, on the other hand, know how much can be lost—the option premiums—but are in the dark as to how much profit might accrue to them.

The degree of risk is reflected in the price. The more in-the-money the option is, the greater the jeopardy to the option writer, so the higher the premium. If the written option is out-of-the-money, the risk is less and so is the premium. Conversely, the purchaser must pay more for an in-the-money option than for one that is out-of-the-money.

Strategies

While the choice of listed options in a class (all the options for a company) can be numerous, with several exercise prices and expiration dates, most successful options are bought or written close to the market price of the underlying security. This reflects the simple market fact of life that the present price is determined by all known information; conversely, the further away in price and time, the greater the uncertainty. The heart of the problem is quite simple: What is a fair price for an option? The answer, for the writer, is an equilibrium price, one that compensates him sufficiently for the loss of opportunity to gain. For the option buyer, a fairly priced option is one that affords a chance to gain for a reasonable premium.

When translated into dollars, option premiums usually range between 8 percent and 12 percent of the underlying security. While there is no absolute percentage figure, recently a six-month call option on IBM at-the-market was 8.5 percent, and a nine-month was 10.5 percent. Puts were 7 percent and 8.5 percent, respectively. And for Dow Chemical, an at-the-market call was 6 percent for six months and 9 percent for nine months, while Tandy puts at the market were 8 percent for six months and 10 percent for nine months.

One option strategy is to write overpriced options and to buy underpriced options. But determining an optimal price is probably no less difficult than determining the value of the stock. Another option strategy is to write call options, in order to reduce risk and tie down a fixed rate of return. If one can earn 8 percent on a six-month option, the annual 16 percent is respectable, especially if the shares themselves are not moving.

Besides a number of complex and convoluted option formulas, there are a variety of hedging techniques. Perhaps the simplest is the "straddle"—the simultaneous buying of a put and a call on the same stock at the same exercise price and the same expiration date. The buyer of a straddle is presuming that the share price will move dramatically one way or the other, but he is unclear as to which way it will be. (Will the oil field come in? Will the strike be settled? Who will win the class action lawsuit?) By paying two premiums, he is secure against the expected volatile move. If he is twice blessed, the price will move violently up and down within the strike period, enabling him to exercise the put on the downswing and the call on the upswing.

For this privilege, he naturally pays two premiums—an expensive admission ticket for this game, since if he is right only once his gain must not just be in-the-money but deep-in-the-money to cover the other premium. The seller of straddles (although frequently the put and call are bought from separate sources) assumes that the price action will be so negligible that the options will not be exercised.

A nine-month straddle on Widget Works at $25 might cost $8 for a call and $7.50 for the put, a total of $15.50 ($1,550). Should the price rise to $35, the call premium will rise to $18 and the put premium will fall to $1. Instead of exercising, the straddle holder terminates or unwinds his position, selling the options for a profit of $3.50, or $350. He could, of course, exercise his call option and let the put option run down until it expired in case the market nose-dived. This way he would gain ten points in the stock transaction, or $1,000 (less commissions), but the initial cost was $15.50 ($1,550). Clearly, he loses by exercising the option, but not by terminating or selling it back to the market. For this reason, most options are terminated rather than exercised. Had the price fallen, the put, rather than the call, would have gained in value, but the arithmetic would have been similar.

There are other put and call option combinations: A "strip" is two puts and one call, bought on the assumption that prices will decrease rather than increase. A "strap" is the opposite—two calls and one put on the same underlying shares at the same price and exercise period. The assumption is that prices are likely to advance rather than retreat. The main thing to bear in mind in all option strategies is the breakeven point. As the combinations increase, so do the premiums (not to mention the potential commissions), and so does the breakeven point. For the writers of such combinations, the premium income on naked writing is doubly enticing, but the open-ended liability in volatile markets may make sleeping difficult.

CHAPTER 6

Commodity Futures

*Economy, n. Purchasing the barrel of whiskey that you do
not need for the price of the cow that you cannot afford.*

—Ambrose Bierce, *The Devil's Dictionary*

"Like a River"

Until very recently, investors and market participants shied away from dealing in futures, monetary contracts to be settled in the weeks or months ahead. However, following the explosion of interest in the listed options market, the financial world has shown a quickening interest in commodity futures and in options on these futures. Broadly speaking, commodities are all "goods and articles . . . in which contracts for future delivery are presently or in the future dealt in." Commodities or futures fall into five general categories: grains and oilseeds, livestock and meat, food and fibers, metals and petroleum, and financials. Traditionally an arcane field best left to professionals, futures have now whetted the public appetite, as these contracts provide great leverage for both protecting assets and speculating.

Commodity futures and forward contracts have always been suspect. Both here and abroad, selling something that either didn't yet belong to you or was not yet produced or created was perceived as vaguely immoral. France outlawed forward contracts in the early 19th century, with Napoleon's support. A French stockbroker nearly succeeded in changing the emperor's mind with the following argument:

> Sire, when my water carrier comes to my door, does he commit a crime if he sells me two barrels when he had but one on hand?
> Certainly not. He is always certain of finding more in the river. Well Sire, consider the Exchange; it is like a river of stock!

In the United States, the same suspicion and skepticism existed long after the establishment of the nation's first commodity market, the Chicago Board of Trade, in 1848. Chief Justice Oliver Wendell Holmes put the issue in proper perspective when he wrote: "In a modern market, contracts are not confined to sales for immediate delivery. People endeavor to forecast the future and to make agreements according to their prophecy. Speculation of this kind by competent men is the self-adjustment of society to the probable."

The public and those innocent of markets presume that the exchanges, regardless of what is being traded, are dens of iniquity. They see little economic justification for commodities markets and, worse, assume that they are being manipulated against the common good. Someone is always making a pile off the back of the consumer. Such thinking is not without some basis in fact. Markets are occasionally abused, lending truth to the argument that they need to be regulated and policed to be kept fair and equitable.

It might be helpful to clarify the nature of futures and forward contracts by examining the nature of speculation. Morality aside, it is the uncertainty of economic life that makes speculation desirable and even necessary for the smooth operation of markets. Rather than acting as a destabilizing force, speculators save the market from unpredictable lurches. Since the outcome of harvests or the demand for industrial minerals cannot be known in advance, speculators enter the market, buying or selling the commodities in anticipation of favorable price action. They act as a buffer.

Naturally, they attempt to be right; but right or wrong, they put their cash between the farmer or producer and the processor or manufacturer. Both the producers of the commodities and the users have their prices fixed and can plan ahead. Both the producers and the users are, in modern economic jargon, risk-averse. Speculators absorb the risk for a price, but the cost to society or to the economy might be far greater if these intermediaries were absent.

If, for example, there were no speculators or commodity exchanges to absorb and spread the risk, prices after a harvest would fall dramatically, due to surpluses, then rise precipitously some months later as storehouses and pipelines emptied. Speculators even out seasonal price changes and, for the price of storage and transportation, make a commodity globally available.

Speculators and exchanges act as middlemen, standing between parties of unequal size so that sheer volume does not upset the market to the detriment of small participants. Some economists argue that speculators increase a trend, destabilizing the market. But others are just as vociferous in maintaining that such action is self-canceling, as it brings in speculators with opposite views. Certainly "corners"—the act of controlling most of the available commodity—can be harmful, but it is rarely done, and the various policing agencies, such as the Commodities Futures Trading Commission, are empowered to prevent it.

Speculators are commonly misperceived as nothing more than gamblers throwing dice. In reality, gamblers and speculators are dissimilar: Gamblers leave their fates to the rules of chance; speculators attempt to amass as much information as possible in order to make a judicious decision. In this sense, they are not different from investors, though their time frame is usually scheduled for more immediate gratification.

There is still another difference between gamblers and speculators. Gamblers create situations in which to wager, from horse races to poker. Speculators create no risks; they attempt to profit from the natural fluctuations in supply and demand. Commodity prices would still fluctuate if no speculators existed—perhaps even more so!

Hedging

Although speculators are integral to the operation of a commodity exchange, the main purpose of the exchange is to provide a hedging mechanism for producers and users, sellers and buyers. The nation's eleven commodity exchanges exist to remove the risk, as much as possible, from commercial enterprises that must deal with pricing decisions based on future events. In the past, commodity exchanges dealt primarily with the staples of everyday existence: corn, wheat, cattle, sugar, butter and eggs, as well as the necessities of an industrial economy, such as cotton, copper, oil, rubber and lumber, among others. In recent years, the exchanges have added new products in a bewildering array: financial futures, foreign currencies, precious metals, stock indexes and options on many of the underlying commodity contracts. Though the products are diverse, the principles remain the same: The exchanges are a way of transferring risk from the business community to the financial world, where it is dealt with more expeditiously.

Businesses wish to fix future costs as much as possible. If a business does not enter into a forward contract, it is conceivable that the commodity it wishes to purchase in three months might be cheaper by then, affording the company a bigger profit. But most businesses are not interested in increasing their profits in such a haphazard way, for it leaves them open to just as haphazard a loss. By entering into a forward contract, a business attempts to fix the cost of its raw materials in the future, knowing full well that in doing so it also gives up any windfall gain.

The same holds true for the producer or dealer; he wishes to set a price now at which he can sell his product in the future, when he has harvested it or inventoried it. In brief, he wishes to protect the ownership of his assets. He enters into a futures contract as a temporary substitute for the concluding transaction to be made in the cash market at a later date. (All futures contracts are standard: Quality and quantity are all fixed by the exchanges, differing only in terms of price and delivery time.)

Both producers and users of commodities wish to hedge against unfavorable trends in prices. Producers usually hedge against lower prices. Consequently, a classic technique is to buy (go long) the commodity for delivery when it is needed, but simultaneously sell (go short) an equal amount of futures contracts for the same time. The basic assumption is that the hedger takes on a position in the futures market that is equal to and opposite a current cash position. This totally hedged position is termed "long the cash" and "short the future." It consists of four separate transactions: A grain operator buys 5,000 bushels of wheat at $4 per bushel on January 2. At the same time, he will sell short one July wheat futures contract (5,000 bushels per contract) at $4.20 per bushel. He has protected himself from price fluctuations even if the price of wheat declines. In June he sells his inventory, the 5,000 bushels, for $3.75 per bushel, a loss of 25 cents per bushel in his cash account. But simultaneously, he buys one July wheat contract at $3.95 per bushel, a gain of 25 cents per bushel in his futures account. He has successfully hedged his operations, neither profiting nor losing from a change in price.

Users usually hedge against higher prices. The user or manufacturer fixes his cost by buying futures contracts. If the product's price goes down, he can always sell the contract and take a loss while offsetting it by buying the needed materials in the lower spot, or cash, market.

Another example might be a copper producer who will mine 1,000 tons of copper during the next six months. Prices are high now, but foreseeable soft business conditions are likely to reduce them. Unable to sell the unmined copper now for cash, the producer sells copper futures (a standard contract is 25,000 pounds). When the copper is mined and sold, the futures contract will be bought back on the commodity exchange. If prices do decline as anticipated, the producer will offset his cash losses with profits from the futures.

These hedges can be used by manufacturers, importers and dealers wherever there is a futures market on raw material or inventory. And those using hedges can be completely or partially hedged and can even cross hedge—use futures on two commodities that are different but price-related, or use multiple hedges within a product and its by-product.

To be more specific, say an importer makes a contract in January to deliver 37,500 pounds of Colombian coffee in June to a local roaster. The roaster agrees to pay $1.50 per pound in January, the current cash, or spot, price. In order to avoid potential loss, she shorts, or sells, one June coffee contract (37,500 pounds) for $1.60. In May she sells the imported coffee but only gets $1.40, a loss of 10 cents a pound, or $3,750. But at the same time she buys the June futures contract for $1.50, a gain of 10 cents a pound, thus canceling out the loss. This is a perfect hedge, and it presumes that cash and futures prices move together so that the gain in one offsets the loss in the other.

Since the world is not perfect, cash and futures prices sometimes diverge during the life of a contract, though they tend to converge by the settlement date. This difference between cash and futures prices is called the basis, or the basis risk. (It is commonly defined as the cash price minus the futures price.) The hedger builds the hedge on the basis, replacing the basis risk with the price risk—changes that can be anticipated and changes that are unexpected. The basis risk always remains; the purpose is to eliminate the price risk. If the two are too far out of line, the hedge may not be worthwhile. Hedges are not so much concerned with price trends as with the spread between spot and futures prices.

Speculators and Traders

Most participants in the commodity exchanges are not producers or users, sellers or buyers; they are speculators and traders rather than hedgers. Of all the commodity contracts entered into, only 3 percent to 5 percent of them are delivered or completed. Speculators enter the market to make a profit on the fluctuations, not to protect assets or positions acquired through the normal course of business. In that sense, they take opposite positions to the hedgers, and consequently they have no cash position and no basis risk to be concerned about.

When a speculator enters the market and establishes a futures contract, she increases the open interest (the number of futures contracts outstanding) in that commodity by one and conversely reduces open interest by one when she unwinds or closes out her position. Most producing hedgers wish to protect their crop or commodity from falling prices. Consequently, hedgers guarantee forward prices by selling futures contracts short. Speculators take the other side and usually hold long positions. Thus, a speculator who believes that pork prices will be higher next winter might buy a pork bellies contract (40,000 pounds) or live hogs (40,000 pounds). If she buys the bellies at 75 cents and sells them three months later for 85 cents, she profits by 10 cents a pound, or $4,000. The person selling the contract loses $4,000.

At the time of a transaction, the price reflects a distillation of the best information in the industry. It attempts to account for all supply-and-demand factors, the price of feed grain, Department of Agriculture reports and forecasts, the cycle of hog production, previous carryover, even the bearing of interest rates. Speculators must digest all this price information before jumping in.

In another category of players are the arbitrageurs, who buy and sell the same commodity almost simultaneously to take advantage of temporary small price differentials. They tend to iron out price fluctuations and step in when the traditional limits or relationships between cash and futures prices get out of hand. Should the futures price exceed the cash price by more than the carrying or storage charges and the normal basis spread, the arbitrageur will step in and sell the futures and buy the cash product to hold for delivery. Her profit is usually quite small, but often dependably sure.

There are other characters in the cast: floor traders, day traders, scalpers, and brokers or commission merchants. In recent years, the investing and speculating public has come into these markets with a vengeance. Much of the increase in this volume can be attributed to the new exotic commodities and options on them.

A commodities account is somewhat different from a brokerage account in stocks and bonds. The difference stems from the nature of commodity transactions. Trading in futures for the speculator is trading in an item for promised delivery. Actual legal title to the goods passes only upon de-

livery, and since more than 95 percent of all forward contracts are closed out before delivery, there is no need to put
up cash for the value of the contract. What is required is
earnest money, termed *margin*, to ensure that the purchaser
will fulfill her obligations. *Margin* payments for shares is a
down payment, with the broker lending the customer (at interest) the difference for the purchased securities. Margin for
commodities is good faith money; no other financing is necessary. Nevertheless, the customer is fully liable for losses
above and beyond her margin money.

One of the major attractions of commodity trading is its
great leverage. Though it differs from commodity to commodity, most futures require a margin payment of between 5
percent and 10 percent of the contract's value. Thus a 50,000-
pound contract for cotton, when the spot price is 75 cents, is
$3,750. For each 1-cent change in the commodity price, the
contract value changes by $500. Clearly, a fluctuation of a
few cents would put the margin in jeopardy. Every commodity has established limits for the maximum allowable daily
change in price. For cotton it is 2 cents a pound, which means
that the maximum a cotton contract can change in price in a
given day is $1,000. The maximum limits on some commodi-
ties are fairly low—oats is $300—but gold and silver have a
maximum of $2,500.

In opening a commodities account, brokerage houses usually require greater margin maintenance than the minimum
margin levels set by the commodity exchanges. More than
that, they usually require proof of substantial assets and/or
the ability to absorb risk. Price action on commodity markets, almost without exception, can be extraordinarily volatile for a number of reasons: Markets are thin, there is no
specialist maintaining a book of orders to lend a cushion to
adverse market moves, and prices are determined by open
outcry in the pits of the exchanges—all of which is under-
scored by leverage and margin calls. The result is that any
speculator or trader must constantly monitor her positions.
An unexpected storm during the harvest season, a failure or
default by a major international bank, the breakout of hostilities in deepest Africa—any and all can send markets roaring
through the roof or into a tailspin to the daily limits. There is

no "one decision" commodity for all seasons, nothing you can buy and put away.

One common fear among novice commodity traders is the nightmare of forgetting a position and finding 50,000 pounds of Maine potatoes marked for sidewalk delivery. Futures contracts are essentially financial transactions to be settled in the last month of the contract. If a futures trader wanted delivery, he would have to close out the contract at the spot or cash price and then go through a series of steps before obtaining warehouse receipts for the stored commodity. In short, the danger is more imagined than real.

Commodity	Standard Contract Unit	1-Cent Change Equals
Grains & Oilseeds		
Wheat	5,000 bushels	$50
Corn	5,000 bushels	$50
Oats	5,000 bushels	$50
Soybeans	5,000 bushels	$50
Soybean Oil	60,000 pounds	$600
Soybean Meal	100 tons	$1
Livestock & Meat		
Cattle, Feeder	50,000 pounds	$500
Cattle, Live	40,000 pounds	$400
Pork Bellies	40,000 pounds	$400
Hogs, Live	40,000 pounds	$400
Foods & Fibers		
Coffee	37,500 pounds	$375
Cocoa	10 metric tons	$1,000
Sugar	112,000 pounds	$1,120
Orange Juice	15,000 pounds	$150
Potatoes (Maine)	50,000 pounds	$500
Cotton	50,000 pounds	$500
Lumber	160,000 board feet	$1.60
Metals		
Copper	25,000 pounds	$250
Gold	100 ounces	$1
Platinum	50 ounces	$0.50
Silver	5,000 ounces	$50

One way of playing the commodity game is through a mutual fund or private pooled account (an unregistered fund of 35 or fewer participants). There is much to recommend this approach, since it tempers some of the volatility in a hectic arena. Managed commodity funds provide product diversity, an end to impatient margin calls, and of course professional expertise. It is part of the proverbial wisdom in the commodity world that "futures traders lose money because they can only afford to trade a few commodities at a time." Managed accounts end that problem, which explains their rapid growth and popularity. While most of registered managed futures funds were started to deal in traditional commodities, a whole new era was dawning; financial futures, foreign currencies, stock indexes and options on indexes are all areas ready to be exploited.

Financial Futures

Since their inception in 1975, financial futures—chiefly U.S. Treasury bills and bonds—have shown spectacular growth, and they are now the most widely traded futures in the world, exceeding the cash market in these obligations by several times. Such futures can be either a source of income or a defensive tool to protect against interest rate risk. Besides Treasury obligations, futures markets have also sprung up in certificates of deposit, Eurodollars and stock indexes, but the underlying principles remain the same as for dealing in agricultural commodities. These futures contracts are simply commitments to buy or sell a financial instrument for a certain price during a specific time period. Markets are made in the exchange pits by open, competitive outcry; no market maker is involved.

The basic unit for Treasury bonds, the most widely traded futures, is $100,000 of face value (though there is a mini contract of $50,000). Trading in financial futures requires the deposit of margin, 4 percent to 5 percent of the face value: Initial margin for the contract is $2,400 plus $1,500 or $2,000 maintenance margin. Prices on futures are quoted in the same way as the underlying government debt—in a percentage of par value (e.g., 94–01 or 94½, which translates into $943.125). The minimum price fluctuations are in ½ of a point, or $1,000 ÷ 32 = $31.25. Daily price fluctuations are limited to $2,000 per contract, or 64/32 above or below the previous day's settlement price.

Delivery of the actual debt instrument is possible (the futures bond contract is based on an 8 percent coupon with at least 15 years to maturity or call) with a specific set of conversion factors for bonds that are different from the set yield and maturity of the contract. In reality, less than .5 percent of T-bond futures are delivered; most contracts are liquidated by offsetting trades, either by selling the same number of bond contracts in the same month or, if short, by buying the same number of bond contracts for the same month.

Like all commodity contracts, financial futures are used to hedge risk: Owners of government and nongovernment debt wish to protect themselves from the vagaries of interest rate fluctuations. Financial futures allow these hedgers (usually commercial and financial institutions, along with private citizens) to transfer some of that risk to speculators. Naturally, speculators have distinct ideas about the trends of interest rates and take positions accordingly.

Let's look at a typical short hedge on the Chicago Board of Trade. An investor owns $100,000 worth of 11¾ percent Treasury bonds with a current market price of 117²³/₃₂, yielding 9.89 percent. The owner is afraid that interest rates will increase and the value of his bonds fall, so he decides to hedge by going short. He sells one contract at a price of 83⁵/₃₂. In a few months his prediction is fulfilled and rising interest rates lower the price of his bonds to 104¹³/₃₂, yielding 11.24 percent. But the price of the futures contract has fallen to 74⁹/₃₂. At this point he decides to unwind his position. The result is that he has lost $13,343 in the cash bonds but has gained $8,906 in the futures—a net loss to be sure, but one that offsets two-thirds of the loss in the cash market. The higher-yielding bond fell proportionately more than the lower-yielding (8 percent) futures hedge. This can be offset (for larger positions) by using the conversion factor to calculate how many more of the futures contracts would have had to be sold for total hedge coverage, known as a weighted short hedge. The

Chicago Board of Options Exchange deals in $100,000 face value contracts, but also in $20,000 face value contracts for smaller traders.

Financial Futures	Unit of Exchange
Certificates of Deposit	$1,000,000
Eurodollars	$1,000,000
Ginnie Maes	$100,000
Treasury Bills	$1,000,000
Treasury Bonds	$100,000
Treasury Notes	$100,000

There are other strategies, too, but all tactics reflect credit conditions and interest rates. Sometimes it is most profitable to do nothing; that is, to leave an interest rate exposure uncovered. The cost of a hedge may not make it worthwhile. To be successful with financial futures, a hedger or speculator must understand the nature of the yield curve and anticipate its direction.

Foreign Currency

The exchanging of foreign currencies is as old as trade; in fact, currency dealers like to think of it as the second oldest profession. Well-established markets for moneychanging have existed in every major trading city in the world since ancient Phoenicia. However, in the last decade there has been a maelstrom of activity as world currencies gyrated wildly due to wars, inflations, recessions, revolutions and beggar-thy-neighbor trade practices.

From the 1945 agreement at Bretton Woods to 1973, the major trading currencies were locked into a system of fixed exchange rates, with an anchor of gold at $35 per ounce. Central banks stepped in with elaborate swaps whenever there was a threat of a run against a currency. But by 1971 there were so many greenbacks abroad due to the Vietnam War and the inflation generated by it—along with an overly favorable balance of trade and the corporate invasion of Europe—that it was no longer possible for foreign holders to redeem dollars for gold. With the gold window slammed shut, currencies were cut adrift. After the first devaluation of the dollar in 1971 and the second in 1973, currencies were subjected to the speculative tides as they floated freely.

In the 1970s, America witnessed enormous growth in its foreign trade: In one decade its exports moved from 9 percent of the GNP to more than 20 percent. This combination of dollar devaluation and the growth of foreign trade dealings made for hectic activity in the currency markets; private citizens were attempting to protect their financial assets from shrinking while importers and exporters, manufacturers, foreign subsidiaries and dealers in foreign securities were busy buying and selling yen, marks, pounds and francs.

This globalization of markets, abetted by the telecommunications explosion in the 1980s and 1990s lent an instantaneous transactional element to this free-floating currency world. By the beginning of 1995 it was estimated that one trillion dollars passed through the foreign exchange markets daily. Most of these transactions are institutional, but individual investors are not excluded.

Anyone needing to make a transaction in a foreign currency can do it in the spot or cash market by walking into a commercial bank or currency dealer to buy or sell currencies. Thus, in the daily listing in the financial pages for Foreign Exchange, one can find the daily trading prices of major currencies, from the Austrian schilling to the Venezuelan bolivar. For anyone wishing to purchase or sell foreign currency in the future, banks will, for a small commission, enter into forward contracts.

For example, an exporter has sold a shipment of personal computers to the United Kingdom against payment in three months. The bill for $500,000 will be paid by the British importer in pounds sterling. The American exporter wishes to protect his payment and enters into an agreement with his bank to exchange the pounds at a rate of $1.60 per pound, close to its present spot value. The exporter has now hedged his exposure to currency fluctuations and has eliminated any foreign exchange risk. He has pinned down a 33 percent profit, which might otherwise have disappeared had the pound subsequently sunk to $1.05, as it did in 1985. The bank tailored a forward contract specifically for him both in time and amount. An importer who needed foreign currency to pay for a shipment in a few months could have done the same thing, entered into a forward contract to buy a foreign currency at a fixed price for delivery.

Currency rates are extremely sensitive and fluctuate significantly, especially since currencies are no longer stabilized around fixed rates. (Some European currencies are loosely tied together by the European Monetary Union, but that does not stop individual ones from fluctuating against the dollar.)

The most recent demonstration of wild currency gyrations was illustrated by the Mexican debacle which unfolded after that government devalued the peso in December 1994. Although the first official devaluation was relatively modest, only 15 percent, initially it did draw attention to the precarious state of Mexico's finances and its heavy reliance on foreign funds for development. Once the devaluation took effect, foreign investors and money managers awoke to the fact that a change of president, two political assassinations, and a peasant rebellion were not the stuff of stability and confidence. Everyone rushed for the exits: the Mexican bolsa dropped dramatically—the largest company, Telefonos de Mexico, losing two-thirds of its value. Eventually the peso fell by more than 50 percent. Only after the U.S. cobbled together a $50 billion aid package with the World Bank did some semblance of order return. But in the interim, emerging markets all over Latin America (and even elsewhere) suffered, being tarred by the same brush. For awhile, wits called them "submerging markets."

Nor did the U.S. dollar escape. The image of the leading debtor country extending loans to its neighboring mendicant was thought to be an exercise in hubris. And when concurrently the venerable British investment bank, Baring, went belly up due to misplaced bets on the Japanese futures markets, the dollar fell to new lows against the German mark and the Japanese yen.

Perhaps no better example is needed of the integration of the world currency markets than the Mexican disaster. Naturally, it is virtually impossible to tell where the next crisis will arise, or for what reason.

The fall of oil prices and the weakening of OPEC, poor trade performance and a weakening balance of payments, protectionist measures, the election of a socialist government—all are recent events that have shaken currencies. Interest rates are another major factor with a constant effect on currency levels, and disparities are frequently a cause for interest-sensitive monies to move in order to search out the higher rates. For anyone who deals in foreign currency—be he importer, exporter, business subsidiary, supplier of raw materials, foreign securities investor, interest-sensitive depositor or speculator—there is a double exposure to loss. The first potential loss is on the actual business at hand, and the second is the foreign exchange risk.

With the growth of foreign exchange dealings due to trade and the freely floating exchange rate, futures trading in foreign currencies was introduced in 1972 by the Chicago Mercantile Exchange in its International Monetary Market (IMM). Currency futures are now also traded on the New York Futures Exchange. In some cases they have become an alternative to forward contracts. The IMM Clearing House is, like commodity exchanges, a party to all trades and guarantees performance. And as with other commodity exchanges, customers' accounts are settled every day, thus limiting debt exposure to one day's price action. A futures contract consists of accepting or making delivery of specified amounts of currency on a given date or, as is more usual, making an offsetting purchase or sale of a similar contract before the end of the trading period. Only eight currencies have futures contracts. In order of volume they are: German marks, Japanese yen, Swiss francs, British pounds, Canadian dollars, Mexican pesos, French francs and Australian dollars.

Like commodities, currency futures contracts are highly leveraged: For an initial margin of $2,000, a trader can control 125,000 German marks, worth $87,500 when the mark is 70 cents. When the contract moves 1 cent, the contract value changes by $1,250, which is also the maximum allowable change in contract value each day.

If an American importer buys a March futures contract to pay for merchandise due in three months, the contract becomes more valuable should the exchange rate move from 65 to 70 cents between December and March. The 5-cent increase would represent a gain of $6,250, and the original contract of $81,250 would be worth $87,500. The seller of the contract must now purchase the amount of marks, 125,000, for $87,500 for delivery to the importer. The seller, of course, could have closed out the open position by buying an equivalent contract before the delivery date. On the other hand, the importer or buyer of the contract could have asked for delivery of the marks or could have liquidated the contract by selling it for the profit already reflected in the market price and then purchasing the marks in the spot market.

Besides hedging commercial transactions, financial transactions can also use futures. Should an investor wish to take advantage of interest rate differentials, he could purchase a three-month, £50,000 United Kingdom Treasury bill for $80,000, yielding 10 percent per annum. He expects to make £1,250 ($2,000) in interest. He buys pounds in the spot market at $1.60. In order to safeguard his round trip, he sells a futures contract (£50,000 × £1.605 = $80,250) for three-month delivery to cover his principal when the Treasury bill matures. He has hedged his transaction from exchange loss by selling the pounds at a rate of $1.605 per pound.

If the transaction goes smoothly, at the end of three months his $80,000 worth of British Treasury debt would be worth £50,000, plus accrued interest of £1,250—a total of £51,250, or $82,000 if the exchange rate has remained the same. His futures contract would have been bought in: He would have bought his hedge of £50,000 for a price very close to the spot price, $1.595, or $79,750. While he gained $500 on the exchange rate selling hedge, he has a gain of $2,500 from the total transaction, less commissions.

If the pound had gone down 10 percent in value during his exposure, he would have the same £51,250, but now they would be worth $73,800 ($1.44)—a principal loss of $6,200. However, the futures contract would be bought in: The $82,000 made from the sale of £50,000 could now be closed out by buying the equivalent £50,000 for £1.46, or $73,000, a gain of $9,000 on the selling hedge. Thus the overall transaction would still earn him $2,800. Without the hedge he would have lost the whole $6,200.

Futures contracts on commodity exchanges are not perfect hedges for currency movements. They are limited to eight currencies, with fixed amounts of currency per contract and standard delivery dates. Forward contracts, in contrast, can be written for any currency, for any amount and for any expiration date. Nevertheless, futures have established a special niche for themselves as hedging devices and speculative tools.

Stock Index Futures

Another rapidly growing derivative instrument that has intrigued the financial world is stock index futures. These futures first started trading in 1982; there are now nine separate stock indexes on different commodity exchanges.

Index	Exchange
S&P Composite	Chicago Mercantile
S&P Midcap 400	Chicago Mercantile
Major Market	Chicago Mercantile
NYSE Composite	New York Futures
Value Line	Kansas City Bd. of Trade
Mini Value Line	Kansas City Bd. of Trade
Russell 2000	Chicago Mercantile
Commodity Research Bureau	New York Futures
Nikkei 225	Chicago Mercantile

Futures contracts are primarily financial instruments that create an obligation to buy or sell an underlying item, in this case nothing more concrete than an abstract index. Since there is nothing to take or deliver, all obligations are settled in cash. Participants are hedging positions and/or speculating on trends on the overall performance of the equities markets. As with other futures contracts, a bullish investor will want to trade long index futures, while a bearish one would wish to trade short.

The one common denominator to all these indexes is the contract size: the index times $500. For example, when the S&P 500 is 475, the price of a contract is 475 × $500 =

$237,500. The minimum fluctuation on all exchanges is 5 cents, or $25.00, with daily price limits of five points. While there are settlement dates for each and every contract, ranging from 3 to 15 months, in reality the exchanges balance their books every day in stock index futures. All positions are "marked to the market"—the difference between the contract's value and the previous day's close multiplied by $500. If it is in favor of the investor, money flows into his commodities account; if it is negative, cash flows out. This settlement is not a mere bookkeeping entry, but a daily settling. For example, if a contract holder is short two contracts and the S&P 500 has declined 2½ points for the day, his account will be credited $2,500 ($500 × 2.5 × 2). Consequently, in addition to an initial margin required by the exchanges, commodity brokers require a maintenance or variation margin to cover potential margin calls. The initial margin is something less than 10 percent of the futures value, and the maintenance margin may be another 5 percent. Thus, for less than 10 percent of the contract's value, a participant can enter the market, but margin requirements do differ for hedgers and speculators; less money is required by hedgers since they usually have collateral or cash on deposit.

Stock index futures are perhaps the simplest, most direct, and potentially most popular of all commodity instruments, but they are also the most speculative. Their popularity stems from the fact that the indexes are the answer to that all-pervasive question: "How's the market?" (Indeed, initial attempts to use the Dow Jones Industrial Average, the most widely quoted one, were stymied in court when Dow Jones & Company objected to its use by the Chicago Board of Trade.) The speculative quality is due to the fact that, unlike all other commodities with specific, relevant information that tends to account for major price behavior, indexes are the sum of so much disparate knowledge that there is no meaningful or predictive information with which to foretell general price movements. One study of the S&P 500 Index found that futures correctly anticipated 14 turning points but missed 10 of them—a batting average of .583.

The indexes are all composed of different securities, but they tend to move in a parallel fashion. Some observers suggest that due to their wide range, they are really far better indicators than the Dow Jones Industrial Average of 30 stocks. Both the S&P 500 and the New York Stock Exchange Composite indexes are weighted by market capitalization. In the S&P index there are 400 industrial companies, 40 utilities, 40 financial companies and 20 transportation companies. All the components (a company's price times its outstanding shares) are added up and then averaged. The 1941–43 average base figure was 10. In the New York Stock Exchange Composite Index, all the shares on the New York Stock Exchange are weighted and averaged, as in the S&P; the average was started in 1965 with a base of 50. The Value Line Index, however, is a geometric average of stock price percentage changes rather than dollar values. Nor is the Value Line Index capitalization-weighted; each security carries the same value. The Value Line Index is composed of 1,700 stocks; 855 are Big Board issues, and the remainder are listed on the American Stock Exchange. The net result is not dramatically different, but this index has a reputation of being slightly more volatile than the other two.

There is some feeling among traders that index futures in general tend to be more volatile than the indexes themselves. Nevertheless, index futures are somewhat more predictive in that the difference between futures contracts and the spot price, the basis, remains fairly constant.

Basis risk is related to the cost of holding the commodity contract from its purchase to the settlement date. This carrying charge is calculated on storage costs, insurance and the time value of money. Commodities in which these factors play a role are known as "cost of carry markets." (Pricing patterns of some commodities are less predictable since they rely on market consensus; this is especially true in perishable foodstuffs. These commodities are price discovery markets; the major force is anticipating supply and demand in the future.) In cost of carry commodities, futures can be bought and sold with some confidence that the carrying charges will determine futures prices and that these charges will be kept in line by arbitrageurs.

Like commodities, stock index futures markets tend to be more cost of carry than price discovery markets. But in the cost of carry markets, program traders will sell futures and buy the underlying stock when futures prices are too high, reversing the process by buying futures and selling stock when they are too low. This is easily and frequently done with gold, silver, financial futures and foreign currency, but it is more difficult with indexes since the commission costs of buying and selling all the stocks, or even a rough proxy of the stocks that make up the indexes, would clearly be prohibitive. Thus arbitrageurs and program traders are, at this point, less active in stock index futures, leaving prices to fluctuate around a band. Within that band of overpricing and underpricing are price discovery markets for index futures.

There are half a dozen tactical reasons for using stock index futures. Investors who wish to participate in an upward, bullish surge can purchase futures, and conversely, when the market is on a downswing, they can profit by selling futures. The indexes can also be used as a hedge to portfolios. An investor may wish to keep his long position, but as the bull market matures he may wish to hedge by selling some futures short. Or, on the other side, he may buy long futures to hedge his short portfolio. More specifically, an investor can be apprehensive about the market but still be enamored of a special security: He buys the stock but shorts the futures.

Another use for index futures is to establish a position in the market for relatively little cash. Since timing is all-important to success in the equities markets, indexes enable one to take a position even if funds are not due for a few months. Indeed, foreign investors or Americans who keep funds in foreign currencies can put index futures to good use. A position in futures allows for a substantial position in dollar-denominated equities without the degree of currency exposure an outright stock portfolio would create.

Index futures allow an investor to play the market on two levels, something that was not possible heretofore. One could always buy or sell specific issues, but that had little or nothing to do with the market. Or one could buy a mutual fund, especially an index fund, but at best these were substitutes for the real thing. Now the investor can separate the two by constructing a portfolio based on specific securities, then taking a position based on a purview of the economy and the market at large. By juxtaposing the two, he should be able to optimize portfolio management if he is willing to absorb the contingent risk.

Options on Futures

The latest twist in the commodities markets is options on stock index futures. These are yet another step removed from the underlying securities. In this case, the options give the purchaser the right, but not the obligation (as with commodities), to buy or sell the stock index futures. These options are no different than those on sugar, wheat, gold bullion or financial obligations: Puts give the owner the right to sell the index to the writer of the options contract, and calls give him the right to buy the indexes within the duration of the contract. The prices of these options are also determined in the open market, based on such considerations as the value of the index shares, the length of the option's life and immediate economic prospects. These index options are a hedge on the overall direction of the market as measured by the S&P 500, but also on Eurodollars, foreign currencies, and even on LIBOR (the London Interbank Borrowing Rate).

The options are not tied to index futures, as are the other indexes, but are settled in cash. Options can cost between $200 and $1,200, depending on the length of the life of the contract. The leverage is quite formidable, but since these speculative instruments are still options, the most a trader can lose is the premium of the contract. Whether derivative instruments such as options and futures serve an economic purpose is debatable. While they can provide for hedging, most participants are clearly speculators. As new futures contracts come into being, the investing public will have a chance to indulge every taste. But a caveat is in order: Not all the index futures, or options on indexes or index futures, will work. A number of new futures have not developed a following and have had to be liquidated, such as futures on shrimp, onions and chicken. As a rule of thumb, it is probably prudent to wait until the newest financial instruments have had a trial run of a year or so and to avoid any that are too unusual or exotic. The commodities industry, after suffering years of neglect, has lately been accused of throwing out all sorts of contracts, like spaghetti against a wall, to see which ones will stick. Investors, traders and speculators should avoid getting splattered by the falling pasta.

Derivatives

Of late derivatives are decidedly in the news—and of course much of that news has been bad. A number of high-profile disasters and bankruptcies, allegedly attributed to derivatives, have given them a black eye. Whether the damnation is deserved is problematic. What is not problematic is the enormous role derivatives now play in financial markets around the world.

The first question is to define derivatives—no small task, since they are essentially second-tier instruments, obtaining their value from first-tier underlying elements. For example, an option is a derivative instrument, as we saw in a preceding chapter, obtaining its value from the price of the underlying stock. An option contract, whether a put or call, is a simple derivative. What makes defining derivatives so difficult is the number of instruments that enter into a derivative hedge. Often there are two or more second-tier vehicles playing off against each other, and some of the instruments are based on public market prices, while others are not exchange traded.

The reasons for the explosive growth of derivatives stem from the development of options, futures, currency and interest rate swaps. These instruments met specific needs to hedge one-sided exposure or liability. By hedging, an act that generally entailed being on both sides of a transaction, risk was mitigated.

Two dangers arose from derivatives. The first was to put on a one-sided hedge—one without a countervailing force. The hedging company or institution was then acting as a financial speculator, leaving itself open to more risk than it had anticipated. The second danger arises from the nature of derivative instruments. For them to fulfill their economic function of providing liquidity in these markets, such instruments are usually sold on credit for a small downpayment. This affords enormous leverage, as is the case with futures contracts. Unfortunately, some of the derivative disasters of late occurred because the derivative package was not "marked to market" everyday—as is the case with all contracts traded on American exchanges (but not necessarily on foreign exchanges). This combination of great leverage (or totally unhedged positions) and uncertain if not inflated or proximated prices led to margin calls, forced sales and devastating losses.

Derivative losses among the major players will give an idea as to the diverse nature of the packages. The collapse and bankruptcy of Orange County, California, a $2 billion loss, was due to interest rates. The county treasurer bet that interest rates were headed down in 1994, but the Fed's action of raising short-term federal funds and the discount rate proved that scenario wrong.

Indeed, Orange County had a lot of company in 1994. Many very sophisticated hedge fund managers, international bankers and plain speculators had found what amounted to a free ride for three years preceding 1994. The Fed flooded the world with cheap dollars (through the creation of dollars at low interest rates) to stabilize what was thought to be an endangered banking system due to the savings and loan debacle of the late 1980s. This flood of money did indeed strengthen the banking system, as banks rebuilt their balance sheets. But the money market participants also took advantage of the Fed's largess. They too borrowed heavily at low rates in order to invest in high-yielding instruments, both domestic and foreign. Some of those investments were direct, but since there was more leverage much more was derivative. This free ride on interest-rate differentials was meant to enhance their rate of return.

When interest rates started to climb, the principals—the price of the bonds, whether direct or derivative—started to fall, first gradually and then precipitously. This in turn triggered calls for more margin or for the outright sales of positions.

Many of these participants were private hedge funds, such as Askin Capital, which lost $600 million and was forced into liquidation. Another investment management firm, Piper Capital, a subsidiary of Piper Jaffray, stockbrokers, also stumbled badly, losing $700 million, but was bailed out by its parent. The huge grain company, Cargill, was forced to assist its Minnetonka Fund when it lost $100 million.

All these companies' losses were due to packages of high-yielding mortgage-backed securities. Other forms of derivatives are termed *structured notes.* These were the undoing of Mellon Trust ($250 million) and Bank of America's Pacific Horizon Fund ($68 million).

Still other corporations, such as Procter & Gamble ($157 million), Eastman Kodak ($220 million) and Landis & Gyr ($308 million) were taken to the cleaners, a la Orange County, with interest rate swaps that went sour. Another derivative package, this time dealing in currencies, was the undoing of Kashima Oil ($1.45 billion) and Tokyo Securities ($324 million). And some companies were hurt by currency derivatives, namely Metallgesellschaft AG ($1.35 billion) and Codelco ($200 million).

In short, in the pursuit of raising rates of return (since they were so low in plain vanilla money market funds in the early 1990s), a variety of banks, mutual funds, government agencies and corporations were decimated by derivative instruments. Naturally, law suits, firings, reorganizations and governmental investigations were all consequences of derivatives gone wrong. These investors, due to the complex nature and leverage of these instruments, took far larger losses than they ever anticipated.

Though 1994 saw derivative losses of almost $10 billion, it must be remembered that most derivative instruments worked as planned. No doubt $10 billion is a lot of money, but in a universe estimated to be $35 trillion of derivatives, the losses are fractional. If a Baring's Bank, the oldest merchant bank in Great Britain, does not or will not oversee its traders through the application of risk management tools, then they no longer deserve to survive. Blaming an unsupervised trader for taking undue risks is a form of scapegoating, and blaming the derivative instruments for the failure is a form of killing the messenger. Markets, whether in derivatives or stock, do not necessarily accommodate the greediest, the least informed or the incompetent—nor should they.

Of course it is an ill wind that blows no good. In this case a whole new Wall Street business is being developed to undo the unhappy consequences of failed derivative packages. This is a form of reverse financial engineering. The same Wall Street firms that structured the original packages are now busy "reconstituting" those packages with other derivatives to cancel out their inherent volatility. The final result is a new instrument that is either a fixed rate or a floating rate instrument with far more benign characteristics than the original. They can be resold with less volatility and less anxiety to new institutional holders.

The derivative market is large and complex—not a playground for individual investors, no matter how sophisticated. What most investors want to know is relatively simple, since they are unlikely to be sold a derivative in the first instance. But they might end up buying a derivative instrument unbeknownst to themselves in the context of a mutual fund. Only by reading the fund prospectus (or by calling and asking) can an investor be aware of their presence. Any prospectus that refers to "enhancing yield" or uses borrowed (leveraged) funds is likely to have some derivative exposure. It is then up to the investor to decide whether that risk is his or her cup of tea.

Indeed, some mutual funds were affected by the last derivative debacles in 1994 and 1995—especially the money market funds. In that hotly contested arena, some fund managers attempted to increase yield by buying derivatives instead of the simple, standard instruments that usually constitute the corpus of a money market fund—CDs, Treasury Bills, Bankers' Acceptances or Commercial Paper.

As a consequence, a few funds were forced to "break a buck," that sacrosanct divisor for these funds. Happily, investors were not impacted since the management companies made up the losses in those few cases. The SEC is now actively formulating rules of disclosure for mutual funds. However, their implementation may be some time in the future. And despite the bad press, derivatives are not going to go away.

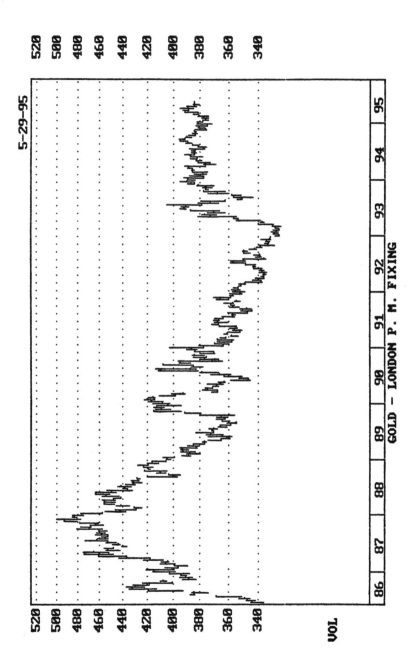

GOLD — LONDON P. M. FIXING

worth about $1,749,888,000,000. To put it another way, all the gold ever mined (since most gold mined has been saved, less an estimated 16 percent thought to be lost or unrecoverable) is roughly equivalent to two-fifths of the annual gross domestic product of the U.S.

If it were all put into one solid cube it would be about the size of a smallish New York City apartment building, some 60 feet by 60 feet by 60 feet.

Where is all this gold presently located? About 30 percent of the hoard rests in the basements of the world's central banks and international depositories as official reserves; 23 percent is in the form of private investment holdings. Most gold has been consumed in gold product consumption—jewelry, teeth, electronic connectors, plating, etc. Each year the gold inventory increases by two or three percent.

On a current basis, the gold offtake (production) in 1993—3,145 metric tons—went into jewelry (79 percent), industrial and other consumption (11 percent), bars (6 percent), and coins (4 percent). Most governments impose some restrictions which discourage gold ownership: Some restrict or prohibit the import and export of gold, while some tax imports or sales and place consumption taxes on gold jewelry. Thus for all the lip service paid to the free gold markets, the World Gold Council estimates that 3.9 billion people in the world, out of a population of 4.8 billion, have difficulty in gaining "unhindered access to gold products that meet their needs."

Of late, demand has grown in the Far East, especially in China where demand nearly doubled from 1990 to 1993, from 120 tons to 223 tons. Clearly the rapid development of the Chinese economy has fostered the demand for gold. With only 1 registered gold retailer for every 400,000 people (compared with Italy where there is 1 for every 4,800 people), the potential for gold sales is vast. And broad inflationary forces in China are likely to further feed the gold frenzy.

These aboveground reserves can exert great pressure on the price of gold, for it is a particularly liquid commodity with virtually 24-hour trading opportunities. Gold's day starts on the other side of the dateline in the Far East, Tokyo and Hong Kong, and works its way to Zurich, Johannesburg, Paris, London, New York and back across the Pacific. While no one knows how much gold is traded daily, some market participants think it is more than $2 billion worth. Nevertheless, the market capitalization of all the gold mining companies relegates it to a rather minor industry. It is the product, not the plant and equipment, that fascinates world markets.

Participants in the gold market fall into two categories: the short-term traders and the long-term investors. The short-term traders are especially active in the futures and options on futures of 100-troy-ounce contracts, in which each 1-cent change in gold alters the value of the contract by $1, and the maximum allowable daily change in the yellow metal is $25 per ounce. Such short-term trading has some impact on the market, but price movements tend to cancel themselves.

The impact of long-term investing, or disinvesting, is more apparent: When Russia sells gold to pay for imported wheat or industrial equipment for the Siberian gas pipelines, when Arab oil states invest their surpluses in gold, when France sells gold to support the franc—all are large-scale national decisions. And on an individual level, when inflation heats up, cautious investors inevitably turn to a storehouse of value and make long-term commitments to the metal. When inflation appears to be under control, they unwind these positions since gold is a sterile investment—earning no interest. Global savers move into gold when political uncertainty becomes apparent or wars erupt uncomfortably close to home. When interest rates rise, higher-yielding securities and money market instruments become more attractive and some people sell gold, even though other investors are simultaneously buying gold as a hedge against inflation. And still other investors at the start of a cyclical business expansion sell their collectibles and hard assets to invest in depressed equities. These profound crosscurrents make it exceedingly difficult to forecast gold's future price movements.

Professional gold investors attempt to evaluate the supply and demand factors, but since only 11 percent of new bullion is designated for industrial uses, it is difficult to obtain an accurate estimate of future demand. Consequently, the "political" character of gold—or, as some say, its "emotional content," "coefficient of anxiety" or "chaos premium"—produces wide price swings. A number of investors and traders have looked at other factors to determine the price. Since Egyptian times, there was thought to be a cosmic correlation between gold and the sun and between silver and the moon. The symbolism could be reduced to a ratio, which in turn became one of the first exchange rates. Since the sun moved around the earth once every 360 days (before Copernicus), and the moon moved around the planet once every 27 days, the ratio was established at 27/360, or 1/13, which was thought to be the correct spread between gold and silver. Indeed, for long stretches of history, that ratio between the two precious metals did obtain. In recent years, the price of the yellow metal has had a stronger connection to black gold— oil. A considerable part of the Arab oil surpluses went to purchase gold since it was considered a surrogate anti-inflationary holding and an indicator of the purchasing power of real wealth. During the heyday of OPEC, the working rule of thumb was that an ounce of gold should sell for 13 times the price of a barrel of oil. Oil may well have fueled inflation, but, ironically, gold was the sole commodity that kept the oil treasuries abreast of inflation.

Owning Gold and Silver

Investors and speculators can choose from half a dozen ways to acquire gold without being fleeced. A number of financial advisers strongly urge that between 5 percent and 20 percent of a portfolio be kept in gold or precious metals as an anchor that will remain stable in financially tumultuous times. But a vote for gold is not quite so simple as it sounds, precisely due to its great value and the care necessary to protect it.

The most common way to own gold is by acquiring jewelry. But jewelry is rarely made of 24 carat (pure) gold, for that state is too soft. So, though fine jewelry is made of 18 carat gold, it is usually far more expensive than the gold content alone is worth, since one is paying for aesthetic considerations and design. The gold content, in a sense, puts a floor on the jewelry's value; only the degree of its beauty determines the ceiling.

For small investors who wish to acquire gold in limited amounts, bullion coins are extraordinarily popular. The South African Krugerrand is exactly one troy ounce, the commonly recognized quotation for gold. (There are 12 troy ounces to the pound rather than 16 avoirdupois ounces.) On purchase, the price is likely to be 3 percent or 5 percent above the last fixing price to cover commission costs.

Some of that premium is redeemable when the coins are sold. Other gold coins are the Mexican gold 50 Peso, a restrike of an older series, which weighs 1.34 troy ounces (especially popular in South America), and the Austrian gold 100 Corona. The Mexican gold Peso is 90 percent pure gold, containing 1.2056 troy ounces of pure gold and other metals to lend hardness. The Austrian gold Corona is a restrike of a 1915 series, and it too is 90 percent pure gold, but since it is somewhat smaller than the Peso it contains only 1.09 troy ounces. In recent years both Canada, with its one-troy-ounce, one-quarter-ounce and one-tenth-ounce Maple Leafs, and the United States, with its one-troy-ounce and one-half-ounce medallions, have joined the marketplace.

Numismatic gold coins are rare items. In addition to the gold value, a purchaser is paying for the rarity and the condition of the coin. American $20 gold coins minted between 1795 and 1933 usually command a premium of 20 percent or 25 percent compared with the simple bullion coins. But such coins are hard for the layman to evaluate, and they are frequently difficult to sell in poor markets or when gold is out of fashion.

Substantial investors may choose to purchase gold bullion, either for delivery or to be held in their name. The cheapest way to buy bullion is in bar form, since commissions are minimal. Bullion is commonly sold in pure 99.95 percent assayed bars bearing the processor's stamp, with the exception of the Russian and Canadian mints, which turn out 99.99 percent pure bullion. The bars come in 400-, 100-, 10-, 5-, and 1-troy-ounce sizes or in 1-kilogram bars (32.15 troy ounces). While the usual trading lot is five 400-troy-ounce bars, banks, foreign exchange dealers, brokers and even department stores are happy to sell the small wafers.

Small investments in gold may be made through convenient gold coin purchases. The U.S. Treasury markets
American Eagles, coins of one full ounce, half ounce, quarter
ounce and one-tenth ounce of gold. The Royal Canadian
mint does likewise, but also has some smaller coins that are
one-fifteenth and one-twentieth of an ounce. In addition, the
Canadian mint coins one-ounce silver, plus a range of platinum coins—all of .9999 purity.

If one does not need physical possession of the bullion, deposit receipts or certificates can be purchased from recognized dealers and banks. The receipts indicate that your gold
is on deposit in a bank, where insurance and other custodial
chores are tended to—all at a modest charge. Gold certificates avoid another problem: The bullion does not have to be
assayed, or evaluated, each time it is traded. A minimum certificate account is usually $2,500.

Though several million gold coins are purchased by Americans every year, most of the dollar trading volume in gold
takes place in the commodity markets in 100-troy-ounce futures contracts. Such contracts are traded on the New York
Commodity Exchange, the International Monetary Market,
and the Chicago Board of Trade. Futures contracts (some
of which have a life as long as 20 months) are especially
volatile; a wrong position can wipe out $2,500 of value in a
single day on a single contract—even one that was entered
into for as little as $1,215 of original margin. Margin calls can
be avoided by having sufficient funds in the trading account
to weather temporary storms or by a "stop-loss" order, in-
structing the broker to sell should the contract drop below an
established price.

Gold futures contracts are usually liquidating financial instruments, as are most commodities futures. Before the expiration of the contract, the position is closed out and the
difference is settled in cash. However, it is possible to take
delivery of gold; in the delivery month, the exchange's clear-
inghouse will require full payment. In return, the purchaser
gets a depository receipt from the bank holding the gold bullion, the 100-troy-ounce bar. If he or she wishes to leave it in
the vault, the bank will charge a storage cost. Or the owner
can simply take the booksize 8.3-pound bar home. Buying

gold through a futures contract can be cheaper than purchasing bullion if the futures contract is at a discount; however, physical delivery will be subject to local sales taxes, which may reduce the advantage.

Thus the financial pages of your newspaper will show a table similar to this one:

FUTURES

Season's		Week's			Net	Open
High	*Low*	*High*	*Low*	*Sett*	*Chg*	*Int*

Metals

Gold

100 troy oz.; dollars per troy oz.

385.50	375.00	Mar	379.00	378.90	381.80	+5.30	3
425.00	374.50	Apr	386.10	378.30	383.10	+5.30	64,051

The first two columns indicate the season's or lifetime's high and low for the March delivery month contract for 100 troy ounces of gold. This is a weekly chart, indicating the week's high and low in the next two columns. The contract settled at week's end at 381.80, indicating a net change in the next column of a +5.30. Since this was a new contract there were only three contracts in the open interest column, compared with the April contract which had 64,051 contracts of open interest.

Gold options, of course, eliminate the possibilities of margin calls since an option is only a right, not an obligation. The most that can be lost is the premium paid for the option. The possibility of gain is, in theory, infinite, limited only by the rise in price and the duration of the option contract.

Besides limiting the risk, gold options provide a highly leveraged profit potential. A gold option for six months might cost 10 percent of the face value of the contract, depending on whether the price was in- or out-of-the-money. But as with other commodity or stock options, a 30 percent move in the price of gold might well show a 200 percent gain in the price of the option. Options that are out-of-the-money and very short-term, both of which are very cheap, are the most highly leveraged and can show extraordinary percentage profits if the buyer catches a sharp move. However, experience shows that most such speculations are doomed to failure.

Whether you are dealing in gold, silver or platinum, the options table in the newspaper will look like this:

PRECIOUS METALS

Silver (1000)—1,000 oz. cents per oz.

	Prev day Call Vol	0		Open Int	127	
(CBOT)	Prev day Put Vol	0		Open Int	90	

Strike		Calls			Puts	
Price	Apr	Jun	Aug	Apr	Jun	Aug
450	no tr	25.0	no op	no op	16.0	no op
500	no tr	7.0	12.0	no tr	no tr	no op

For a 1,000-ounce silver option, the first column is the strike price (in cents per ounce) followed by three columns of call prices for April, June and August, and then the three columns of put prices. Silver options are far less active than gold options.

The equity options tables will have listings for specific options on the major gold mining companies. You can, for a short period and with limited funds, control a round lot of a gold company for a fraction of the underlying shares.

The final way of buying or selling gold is through shares in gold mines. If the price of gold does not appreciate, an investment in bullion or coin is a sterile one since it yields no return. One way of obtaining a yield is through ownership of the mine, which has a high dividend rate to compensate for its relatively short life. There are, of course, other factors that determine yield, such as geography; some observers suggest that yields of companies in risky areas must be higher to compensate investors for that risk.

Mines in North America have lower dividends than South African mines for that very reason. Some of the leading publicly traded North American gold mines are: Placer Dome, Giant Yellowknife, Homestake, Battle Mountain, Echo Bay, Newmont, Freeport McMoran Copper & Gold, American Barrick and Santa Fe Pacific.

Dividends from foreign corporations are sometimes taxed at their source, as with dividends on South African shares. Even after a 15 percent South African withholding tax on dividends declared in dollars (for which U.S. citizens receive a tax credit), the yield on the South African mines tends to range between 10 percent and 20 percent. The higher yields are associated with the medium- or short-life mines. However, high yields can be deceptive; they may indicate not only a short life, but a potential problem in operations. Gold stocks fluctuate because of management capabilities, labor relations, political considerations, the grade of ore and the cost of extraction per ounce. But in the long run, share prices do bear a relationship to the free market price of gold, thus providing a potential capital gain along with dividend income. Some of the most popular South African mines are:

- Long-Life: Driefontein Consolidated, Kloof, Randfontein, Unisel, Vaal Reefs, Western Deep Levels and Winkelhaak
- Medium-Life: Hartebeestfontein and President Steyn
- Short-Life: Free State, Libanon, St. Helena and Western Holding

Most of the reasons for purchasing gold also apply to other precious metals, especially silver. Besides being an inflationary hedge, a storehouse of value and a source of aesthetic satisfaction, silver is subject to greater industrial demand than gold. The supply of silver has gradually fallen while its consumption has steadily increased, so that now they are in rough balance. In recent years, silver has been considered undervalued. In 1980, a corner in the commodity created by the Hunt family of Texas, plus the panic in the gold market, ran the price of silver up to $50 an ounce—a tenfold increase. By 1982 it had fallen back to $6 per ounce, about where it trades today.

Silver futures are available in 1,000 and 5,000 troy ounces, the latter being the most popular, where each 1-cent change in the price alters the contract price by $50, and the maximum allowable daily change in contract value is $2,500. Silver futures are among the most volatile of all commodity contracts. Silver bullion can be bought in 10-, 100-, and 1,000-troy-ounce bars. Some survivalists, those who are busy planning for a postdoomsday existence, prefer bags of silver coins ($1,000 face value, but currently selling for more than $9,000), and these are actively traded on both the spot and forward markets.

CHAPTER 8

The International Scene

The merchant has no country.

—Thomas Jefferson

Foreign Investments

In the 1990s, the move toward a global economy took quantum leaps. First off the mark was NAFTA, the North American Free Trade Act, signed by the U.S., Canada and Mexico. This created a vast open market, a counterweight to the European Union.

The next step was the final signing of the Uruguay Round of GATT, the General Agreement on Tariffs and Trade, after nearly a decade of wrangling. This landmark treaty ended the threat of protectionism and potential trade wars.

While these important international agreements set the tone for international investing and made it less problematic by establishing commercial protocols, tax agreements and financial reciprocity, the art of investing abroad is an old and reciprocal one.

In the early days, xenophobia, the fear of strangers, was the impulse behind George Washington's warning against foreign entanglements in his farewell address and has continued in this country until very recently. A distrust of foreigners has not completely disappeared in all quarters, but American involvement in international politics and business is now so profound that even tidal waves of neoprotectionism and "fair trade" are not likely to alter it. Perhaps one of the clearest indications can be found in international investments. In 1960, the United States had $85 billion in assets and investments abroad; by 1983, the figure was close to ten times that. Or take foreign trade: In 1970, the nation exported 9.2 percent of the GNP; by 1980, fully 20 percent. Today, one out of five jobs is tied to international commerce, a statistic hitherto thought of as appropriate only to island economies like Great Britain's and Japan's. National economies are now tied so closely together that when one trading partner catches cold, the other sneezes. This integration is financial as well as commercial; indeed, countries have been investing in other nations from the age of exploration and the first days of capitalism. Much of the infrastructure of the Western Hemisphere, and of the United States in particular, was financed in 19th-century European capital markets.

After the Second World War, the flow of investments moved dramatically the other way, first with the Marshall Plan in the 1940s and then, in the 1950s and 1960s, with the private investments of corporations and individuals. This culminated in the American challenge, the fear among Europeans that their major corporations and markets would soon be totally dominated by American multinationals. European governments placed some legal obstacles in the way of overly aggressive company takeovers. Meanwhile, the Vietnam War and declining trade surpluses reduced the growth of foreign investments. The dollar continued to weaken in the 1970s. With the price of petroleum skyrocketing and the subsequent recessions (1969–70, 1973–75), foreign portfolio investments were put on the back burner, even though foreign trade and the recycling of OPEC money to foreign nations proceeded apace.

The attraction of international investing picked up throughout the 1980s, especially while the dollar was greatly overvalued. Foreign investments slowed only temporarily for the Gulf War. Subsequently, investment management companies, mutual funds, pension trusts, investment banks and brokers all discovered that the third world had "emerging stock markets." Even the new Russia and the old China started to dabble in capitalism with new bourses.

Part of the reason for the rush to develop capital markets had to do with the state of most nations' finances. Central governments, whether communist Russia, socialist Sweden, chaotic Italy, Islamic Turkey and a host of other countries all found themselves overextended and broke. Privatization, or the sale of the national patrimony, and the raising of capital on the exchanges became the order of the day.

From the investors' point of view, the newly discovered markets had an exotic fascination, even if some of the European exchanges were older than the New York Stock Exchange. The lure of investing abroad could be summed up in six factors:

- higher yield
- faster capital appreciation
- diversification of assets
- fewer regulations
- tax considerations
- cost advantage

Though some of these opportunities had always beckoned, it was not until the physical mechanisms and communication devices were in place that the advantages could be exploited.

For investors wishing to lend money abroad, where rates were higher, the creation of the Eurodollar market in the 1950s certainly facilitated dealings. Originally started in London by a Russian bank, Eurodollars became an enormous pool of funds that remain outside the regulatory restrictions of the Federal Reserve System, the Bank of England, any other central banking system, the International Monetary Fund and the Bank for International Settlements. (Since then, other hard currencies have also been lent abroad—Euromarks, Europounds, Eurofrancs, Euroyen, etc.) This enabled bankers to lend these dollars in the free world market, unrestricted by Regulation Q of the Federal Reserve System. Regulation Q did more to bring about the Eurodollar market than any other single act when it prohibited the payment of interest on demand deposits and set an unnaturally low ceiling on the interest rates of time deposits.

Due to this rule, interest rate differentials favored European banks, which not only received higher rates for their funds but in turn could pay depositors, many of whom were Americans, higher yields. Banks that specialized in Eurodollar loans (usually in amounts above $100,000) were free of any minimum reserve requirements, which also made their costs lower and their margins higher. This satisfied the American and European companies that could borrow (especially the American ones, which were faced with domestic restrictions due to balance-of-payments problems); the offshore banks, which made a handsome profit on nonresident money; and the depositors, who earned more on their funds.

When the world was subjected to a quadrupling of oil prices after the Yom Kippur War and the subsequent oil embargo in 1973, offshore and international banking facilities were especially instrumental in recycling petrodollars to the less-developed nations. This spread the burden of higher oil prices and averted the liquidity crunch everyone feared. Great anxiety was voiced in business and financial circles that the billions of dollars generated by OPEC would destabilize the international financial system, and that banks would be caught in the classic nightmare of lending long from short borrowings. If the OPEC nations wanted their massive funds on demand, bankers would be in an exposed and embarrassed position.

It was perhaps a touch ironic that tne OPEC nations acted very conservatively in managing their funds, realizing full well that a world financial crisis was certainly against their interests and that they would no doubt suffer accordingly. It was the bankers who nearly shot themselves in the foot by lending all too often to nations without the reserves to pay current interest, let alone the principal. In the Eurodollar market (including petrodollars and other offshore loans), there is no bank or lender of last resort, since central banking systems are not responsible for what goes on beyond their jurisdiction. But the international debt crisis was reduced, or maybe just postponed, when the International Monetary Fund stepped in with more loans, and the central banks, particularly the Fed, did not force the banks to write down their nonperforming loans. Had they done so, several leading American banks would have been technically bankrupt since their dubious debts were in excess of their capitalization.

Since those perilous days, the global markets realized that sovereign state loans were not all they were cracked up to be. Contrary to Walter Wriston, head of Citibank, sovereign state loans did frequently fail, cratering many American money center banks just at the time the domestic savings and loan crisis was unraveling. The U.S. Treasury stepped in with guarantees in the form of Brady bonds for those debt holders. Moreover, the Bank for International Settlements increased supervision and reserve requirements for major international banks. With disaster averted, and with some new safeguards in place, the investment world turned aggressively toward overseas investing.

Country and Credit Risks

The crises in international debt simply illustrates that there are two factors that must be evaluated by anyone investing abroad, even if the investment is nothing more than lending dollars to a foreign bank. First, there is the country risk. Dollar accounts in foreign banks can be subjected to some unpleasant shocks if the monetary authorities decide to block those accounts or devalue their currency. The history of foreign investing is unhappily sprinkled with such incidents.

In 1982 Mexico blocked and devalued American dollar deposits in Mexican banks. Unable to pay back its international loans, and needing all the hard currency it could lay its hands on, the Mexican government blocked dollar accounts and forced conversion at a special low exchange rate equivalent to 50 cents on the dollar. American investors, and resident retirees, previously attracted to Mexico because of its high yields, found that overnight they had lost half of the

$12 billion they had in Mexican banks. And sometimes lightning strikes twice. For a few years subsequent to the 1982 devaluation, Americans and other investors were shy, but by the end of the 1980s, with new political leadership and the passage of NAFTA, investors flocked back to Mexico. The Mexican bolsa soared. Telefonos de Mexico went from a few dollars to $75 per share in 1994. In the rush to modernize and create a dynamic market economy, the country borrowed at high rates. The huge foreign debt overwhelmed the economy by the end of 1994, and the peso was devalued. Telefonos went from $75 to $25. As Yogi Berra said, "It was déjà vu all over again."

When the prospects of economies and foreign money centers turn cloudy, the run for the exits can be life threatening. Witness the reversal of Hong Kong's fortunes as the island's long lease approaches its end. When the Chinese showed no immediate interest in negotiating an extension—and, indeed, proposed the termination of British sovereignty—the roof caved in. The perception that the colony's privileged status might end brought on a depression, with a decline in share prices and real estate and the closing of businesses. For example, the shares of Hong Kong Land, a blue chip company and the owner of the famous Mandarin Hotel, fell 80 percent from their previous high. Once the British-Chinese treaty passed, the Hong Kong markets recovered. Now with the end of British rule proximate, markets and businesses have adjusted and remain buoyant. No doubt this comfort is derived from the free-wheeling economy so visible in mainland China.

Whether an investment is in dollars or rupees, there is always the question of credit risk. Is the investment a sound one, whether it be in a tax-shelter condominium, oil well, foreign drug company or multinational? Credit risk implies an appreciation of all the financial factors that make any investment vulnerable.

Investing abroad is clearly a more complicated process than staying at home. An investor undertakes a foreign currency exposure as well as an investment that may lack some of the criteria necessary for him or her to make critical decisions. One of the principal reasons for buying foreign securities is to make more money than one might at home, but that is not always easy, for it requires investment tools and reliable information that is not necessarily readily available.

Over the years, the assumption that foreign investments are more lucrative has occasionally proven accurate. However, markets abroad fluctuate just as they do in the United States—and sometimes more so, because of the narrower bases and thinner markets of foreign bourses. In short, it is always possible to lose money abroad. Since growth rates are not synchronized, economic cycles are in different phases and foreign monetary and fiscal policies are established in accord with national interests, it is understandable that correlations among world markets are imprecise.

Indeed, the markets of late have decoupled from the American locomotive. While it was once true that when the U.S. sneezed other countries caught cold, in the 1990s economic and financial power has been decentralized. Japan and the emerging economies of Asia are certainly a counterweight, as are the players in the European Union. This devolution of power has much to do with American debts and deficits, which in turn have caused the U.S. dollar—the major reserve currency—to weaken dramatically. Moreover, the conscious effort by Washington administrations from the mid-1980s to the present to aid export industries by promoting a cheaper dollar has not passed unnoticed by market participants. In 1995 a flight from the dollar to marks and yen not only marked postwar lows but may be the beginning of the end of the dollar as the sole reserve currency.

This perception of a perpetual weak dollar clearly affects market prices abroad. Some exchanges whose currencies are tied in some fashion to the dollar, such as Argentina, South Korea and the Philippines are more sensitive to dollar fluctuations.

For all the talk of a weak dollar, however, there are some conflicting views indicating that the dollar is not as weak as is generally thought. On a trade-weighted index, the dollar has maintained most of its value vis-à-vis other major trade currencies. And if one looks at another dollar measurement, one favored by the United Nations and international agencies, purchasing parity equivalence finds the dollar significantly undervalued. It is far cheaper to buy a refrigerator in the U.S. with dollars than in Germany with marks.

Emerging market economies contain another hidden risk. Compared with U.S. economic statistics or those of Western Europe and Japan, their published statistics are often both late and unreliable. Many of these countries have no advanced calendars of publishing dates. The recent debacle in Mexico was no doubt aggravated, since it was not forthcoming about its vanishing foreign reserves, its growing indebtedness and its ballooning money supply. Timelier releases might have diminished the crisis.

The Economist published the following table as a guide to emerging-market reliability:

EMERGING-MARKET STATISTICS

	Timeliness	Availability of quarterly GDP	Overall quality of statistics
Hong Kong	21	Yes	A
Singapore	17	Yes	A
South Korea	2	Yes	A
Taiwan	1	Yes	A
Argentina	2	No	B
Mexico	6	Yes	B
Brazil	14	Yes	B−
Thailand	10	No	B−
Indonesia	19	No	C+
China	10	Yes	C
Russia	21	Yes	C

Source: *The Economist*, March 4, 1995.

It is clear that many emerging markets are very volatile. In general they should be approached only if you can tolerate high risk. In the U.S., markets have on average fluctuated by as much as 26 percent per annum; emerging markets can move significantly more than that.

"What makes emerging markets interesting is that an investor never knows whether his money will ever again emerge from the distant lands whence it was sent," remarked *Barron's*. Besides faulty and late statistics, investors have to be ready to deal with rigged markets, corners and other shenanigans which are outlawed in the U.S. and other mature markets. Emerging markets are clearly not for the timid, but the rewards may well be worth the risks.

Mature global markets may be a better bet for the less adventuresome. These markets are better regulated (there are current attempts to set international accounting standards), broader in that they have populations which are shareholders, and offer fewer problems with liquidity. Nevertheless, scandals are not unknown in Milan, or government influence in Tokyo. International investors must expect the unexpected—but that is the price of finding the next great foreign stock.

Buying Overseas at Home

There are a number of different ways to purchase a foreign interest without leaving home. The simplest way is to purchase shares of an American company with substantial interests in a foreign country. Contrary to practices of a decade or two ago, many companies now break out their foreign earnings since it is a selling point for individuals and institutions. For example, Coca Cola and Pepsico are candid about their overseas revenues. While companies with significant operations abroad are naturally eager to increase profits from these sales, there is a problem: dollar value fluctuations against other currencies can translate into either unexpected profits or losses. A cheap dollar makes foreign sales very profitable, but an expensive one can reduce homegrown profits.

This may not be a consideration for companies with only five or ten percent of their revenues from foreign sales, but it can clearly be one for companies like McDonalds or Coca Cola where half the profits tend to be generated overseas.

Another way of investing abroad without leaving home is through foreign companies whose shares are traded on American exchanges or over-the-counter. There are over 150 major foreign corporations listed for trading directly on the

New York Stock Exchange, such as Royal Dutch Petroleum, the second largest oil company in the world, and Unilever, the giant Anglo-Dutch enterprise. These companies have fully complied with the Securities and Exchange Commission and the New York Stock Exchange listing requirements. There are also companies whose surrogate shares are traded largely in the OTC market. These substitute shares are termed American depositary receipts (ADRs), and they too are registered with the SEC, but some disclosure information is not required. The idea of these ADRs developed in the 1920s, with the first wave of foreign investments. Instead of sending the purchased shares back to the new American owner, a foreign bank (or an overseas branch affiliate or correspondent of a domestic bank) acts as custodian. The bank abroad takes in the security—frequently a bearer share with dividend coupons attached—and an American bank issues an ADR in its place. The ADR may be issued on a one-to-one basis, or, in order to make the trading price comparable to American prices, one ADR may be issued for two, five or ten foreign shares. In the case of high-priced foreign shares, the process is reversed. For example, Novo Nordisk of Denmark, a leading producer of enzymes and insulin, has five ADRs for each of its shares. These negotiable receipts are then traded in the American market, while the custodian takes care of dividends and rights offerings. These ADRs are a convenient way of holding foreign shares and are used by arbitrageurs to take advantage of price differentials in various markets. Some investors prefer to go straight to the source and purchase foreign securities from foreign brokers or banks. There are either no ADRs on the desired shares or the investor prefers to keep the shares overseas. Many foreign shares cannot be solicited in the United States since they do not provide for full disclosure and consequently violate state blue-sky laws. Foreign purchases may save some commission costs, but the mechanics can be confusing and information on dividends, rights and earnings downright scanty on companies that are not well known.

Indeed, the international markets are two-way streets. Foreigners view the United States as a bastion of safety, political stability and economic strength (not to mention a haven from onerous taxation and occasional devaluation or expropriation of funds), even during prolonged recessions. Sophisticated foreigners have always earmarked a portion of their portfolio investments for the United States, along with investments in real estate and farmland. But this inward flow of funds is more than offset by the flow of American money abroad. Recently, Americans have been buying more than $40 billion of foreign securities every year.

Foreign markets have their own idiosyncratic qualities, reflecting national character, the nature of publicly owned companies, trading patterns and settlement mechanisms. European exchanges are several centuries old; the first was probably established in the Netherlands in the 15th century. A Bruges merchant named Van de Beurse ran a small exchange and pawn shop, marked by three symbolic purses (or beurs in Dutch) on a street sign. Beurse's fame spread, and before long the French established a bourse, the Germans a Borse, the Danes a bors, the Italians a borsa, and the Spanish a bolsa. The London exchange arrived somewhat later, settling into 17th-century coffee houses for stock trading. Throughout early modern history, markets on both sides of the Channel flourished. Both the Dutch and the English were creators of joint stock companies, a legal device developed to share in the venture capital opportunities of the day, overseas trading companies.

As mechanisms for capital accumulation, the European exchanges served their initial purpose, but they could not (and even today cannot) be accused of being temples of capitalism for the masses. The European exchanges cater to wealthy investors and financial institutions. In the United States there are 51 million direct stockholders, one of every five citizens; in England the ratio is half that and on the Continent only a quarter. In the rest of the world it varies dramatically. For all the OPEC money, the Arab countries have small and unstable markets, whether they be in Riyad or Kuwait. Israel has an active investing public, as do South Africa and Australia. But it is Hong Kong and Japan that have exploded in size and activity in the last generation. The Japanese have the world's highest savings rate, as much as 22 percent of disposable income (compared with 4 percent in the United

States). This fact helps explain one of the fundamental strengths of the Japanese economy. And these savings end up financing industry through the banks and the markets. On occasion, the Tokyo market trades one billion (low-priced) shares a day.

Consequently, the breadth of public participation, as well as the politicizing of the economy and the structure of financial markets, has much to do with the nature of foreign markets. Where there is a relatively small shareowning public, as in Spain and Italy, prices move erratically. Where financial markets are dominated by banks, as in Switzerland and Israel, prices move at the behest of those financial interests. Where ruling governments are frequently hostile to free enterprise, such as in Sweden and France, the public avoids investing in certain companies that may be on the nationalization hit list—and, of course, are unable to invest in the large companies that are already nationalized. However, in the last few years the drive to privatization has left the investing public somewhat ambivalent. All too often the utility or industry being privatized has performed less than splendidly; only the hope that new management will vitalize a moribund business makes such privatization sales possible.

All of this is by way of indicating that while it is not easy to be right in one's own market, it can be downright difficult to be right in somebody else's backyard. But by staying with well-known companies, it is possible to diversify a portfolio and increase the rate of return. Anyone who had the foresight to buy Sony (Japan), Club Med (France), L. M. Ericsson (Sweden), Broken Hill Proprietary (Australia) or Philips NV (Netherlands), to name just a few, can appreciate that premise.

Euromoney

Although London is the major market for international bonds and loans outside the United States, the City (the British Wall Street) is no longer the center of the financial world. Both New York and Tokyo trade far greater volumes of securities—not surprisingly, considering that both economies are larger than that of the United Kingdom. Moreover, the English disease of "stagflation" has been endemic to its economy for a generation. Still, the City plays a significant role in global finance; reinsurance, gold fixing, currencies, and commodities are all markets with vast impact. Though the London Stock Exchange does not dominate volume trading, it claims to trade the broadest number of shares, handling any stock from any exchange. In the international loan market, the London Interbank Offered Rate (LIBOR) is the cynosure for lending. Since close to $150 billion of international loans are negotiated yearly, LIBOR is a critical guide to the cost of money, as important in the international scene as the prime rate is in the United States.

Europeans are less equity-oriented than Americans. They would rather lend money than invest in shares of corporations. As a result of this conservative predisposition, companies from around the world, including American ones, have plunged into the Eurobond market, where the borrowing costs are somewhat lower and the yields to lenders somewhat higher. An international syndicate brings out a bond issue that is often sold simultaneously in several countries and in different currencies. Most of the corporate issues are straight debt, but a number have special features, such as a payoff in the currency of one's choice, at a fixed rate of exchange, or in gold. Others are zero-coupon issues; that is, they are sold at a deep discount from the face value and pay no periodic income. The appreciation over the life of the bond will equal the sum of the annual interest payments that would have been paid on a regular debt instrument plus the income from compounding those theoretical interest payments. These issues can be purchased by Americans abroad or through domestic sources.

Though especially conscious of yield, worldwide bond buyers are not above participating in strong equities markets. Eurobond marketers developed still another hybrid: a bond with warrants to purchase common stock of the borrowing company. For example, a Swiss bank will issue a $100 million, seven-year bond with warrants at par bearing a 7 percent rate. The warrants, which are detachable, give the right to buy shares at a set price. Investors get a fixed return plus the opportunity to buy a certain number of the bank's shares. These dollar bonds with warrants are in bearer form.

Another twist on the Eurobond market is the practice of selling partly paid debt issues, especially American ones. Investors buy dollar-denominated Eurobonds, but instead of paying for the whole bond, they need make only a 30 percent down payment. These have been particularly popular among foreign investors, who like the stability and strength of American corporations but suspect that the dollar is overvalued. They can take an initial position, and if the dollar declines as expected against their own currency, they can purchase the remaining 70 percent at what amounts to a discount. Another fillip to these partly paid issues is that should the bond's price rise significantly, the buyer can take a disproportionate capital gain on his down payment. These partly paid bonds are issued for national debt as well as for American corporations.

Both the zero-coupon bond and the partly paid bond are recent innovations in the Eurobond market, made at the demand of lenders. Of course, the whole Eurodollar-Eurobond market developed as a way to provide international liquidity, to provide for the recycling of petrodollars and to provide a way for banks to profit outside domestic regulations. And inevitably the international debt crisis—of national states unable to meet their obligations—is directly tied to the vast, ungoverned and unregulated pool of Eurodollars. The presumption among sophisticated bank lending officers that sovereign states would never default, since they would thereby rule themselves out of the international credit markets forevermore, has some validity to it. But a number of banks are overextended on foreign country loans, and within recent memory several have run into trouble, some of it terminal. Sovereign state debt is no guarantee that every government will honor every debt made by previous governments, a fact to which the Foreign Bondholders Protective Council can attest. And devotees of bizarre wallpaper can purchase for pennies the intaglio certificates of Russian Kerenski Loan 5 percent of 1917 or of Chinese Imperial Railway 5 percent Gold Loan of 1907.

CHAPTER 9

Security Analysis

Experience is the name everyone gives to their mistakes.

—Oscar Wilde

Modern Portfolio Theories

Making sense of financial news is more than understanding the mechanics of the marketplace, however important that is. The mechanisms do not work in a vacuum but in a context of ideas, theories and concepts. These ideas are sometimes right and sometimes wrong; about the only sure thing is that they constantly change, reflecting the shifts and transitions of the economic scene.

In recent years, financial markets have seen much of that change—some frivolous and some of lasting import. Investment philosophies are legion—from the one-decision stock to the "nifty fifty," from imitating the indexes to the forecasting technicalities of modern portfolio theory, from contrarian and cyclical behavior to astrology and sunspots. Even the most arcane theories have their promoters and followers.

Still, despite the fickleness of market fashions and the curious practices of some of its participants, the securities markets operate in a far more professional manner now than they did a generation ago, basing their techniques on knowledge and research. The information comes from the financial community as well as from the academic world, the publishing and communications industries, businesses, trade organizations and the government.

Indeed, the flood of information threatens to drown even the most avid. Market participants must be extraordinarily selective in what they monitor, and then attempt to put that information in a workable or useful context. How one views markets is every bit as important as what one hears and sees.

Traditionally, observers and participants are divided into two groups, the fundamentalists and the technicians. For years, the fundamentalist outlook dominated the scene and in a sense still does; few professional money managers will purchase securities of companies that are unknown to them. They want to know all the basics of the operation, from its share of the market to the next generation of products, from its present cash flow to its projected earnings. All are grist for the fundamentalists' mills.

However, some market players gladly ignore these fundamentals. They don't care what the company makes, who manages it or even if it is profitable. The only important element is the action; the trading patterns of the shares is all-important to these technicians. Sheer technical analysis is best done in isolation, without any knowledge of the day-to-day operations of the company itself.

Of late, technical analysis has gathered a strong following. Investors and money managers who would never use it alone are finding it a helpful adjunct in making decisions. And even if they do not incorporate technical analysis into their immediate judgments, they are usually aware of its ramifications or impact. In brief, it is virtually impossible to understand market activity without being aware of this aspect of trading.

The Fundamentalists

But first, let's look at the major elements of the fundamentalists' creed. The securities markets are anticipatory mechanisms, tending to adjust current prices to conform to perceived future circumstances. One can get a leg up by analyzing the elements of corporate finance that make up the future before anyone else appreciates them and/or by doing it more perceptively than anyone else. There are, of course, a variety of factors that come into play in financial analysis and any number of theories about which combination of them will reveal the truth. The truth to be ascertained is the real value of the securities in question. In short, fundamental analysis of corporate figures will reveal how much a company is worth and whether or not this value is presently reflected in the marketplace. Fundamental analysis is meant to answer two simple questions: Is it worth the current price, or more, or less? Furthermore, how does an investment in this security compare with investments in other financial assets?

While a number of variations exist, there are just a few principal methods for evaluating common stock. The one that has received a great deal of academic support in business schools is the "future stream of dividends" model: The total of all future dividends determines the present value of the shares. By adding up all the estimated dividends for a fixed period, say ten years, or for a foreseeable future, one arrives at a rough value of the shares. This method can be refined by discounting the value of the dividends, perhaps by 8 percent, so that next year's dollar in dividends will be worth only 92.5 cents. (The discounting rate can be either the expected interest rate or the expected rate of return on other assets of a similar risk.) The principle of discounting future value is quite valid since the dollar in one's pocket is clearly worth more than the dollar to be received one, two or three years into the future. This future stream of dividends is based on a simple theory—a share is worth only what you can get out of it!

There are a number of problems with this approach even if one assumes that the eventual sale price is the premium for holding the risk attendant to the common stock. While one can reasonably predict earnings and dividends for a year or two, beyond that it becomes little more than a guessing game. Are the shares to be held in perpetuity? That would certainly inflate present value, though it might be a disastrous investment policy simply for the sake of justifying the present value's purchase price. Increasingly, dividend policies of corporations are subject to economic pressures undreamt of a few years ago. As a result, they are unreliable guides to present, let alone future, value.

Since 1960, there has been a dramatic shift in yields. Heretofore, dividend rates could be compared with yields on fixed interest securities. Since stocks were riskier, higher dividend rates were necessary to compensate for that risk. If bonds yielded 3 percent, then equity should return 5 percent or 6 percent. Today, all that has been turned on its head. Dividend payout on the Dow Jones Industrial Average on June 1, 1995 was 2.53 percent, while the yield on ten Dow Jones Industrial bonds was 7.50 percent—a stock-bond yield gap of –4.97 percent. The role of dividends in a period of high interest rates has markedly changed. Furthermore, a variety of growth companies declare no dividends, but reinvest all their earnings back into the company. The future stream of dividends theory of ascertaining present value is logical but impractical and out of date.

Therefore many analysts now use earnings as a base for both their valuation models and their predictions of price trends. Unlike Chippendale desks, Impressionist paintings and Chinese ceramics, the financial assets of corporations have little intrinsic value alone but are of great value when working profitably together. The earnings generated by a corporation are, in a sense, a moving target; it is difficult to measure them with precision and even more difficult to predict what they will be three, six or twelve months into the future.

Given that each company measures it earnings somewhat differently, the single most commonly used analytical tool for determining value is the price-earnings ratio. Earnings that are published in the financial press are, naturally, trailing figures. (Thus, when a company earns $2 for the last 12 months and is selling for $20, the price-earnings ratio is 10.) It is this stream of earnings, expressed as earnings per share, that is the most important figure in determining the rate of corporate growth. What kind of incremental pattern has emerged over the past few years, or even the last few quarters? If earnings have increased by 5 percent annually, the showing is mediocre; by 10 percent, the results are good; but by more than 20 percent they become exceptional. If the pattern has been intact for awhile, this fact alone shows superior management and is a likely indication of value.

While a pattern of increased earnings is highly desirable, it is not current earnings but future projections that are most important in security analysis. How will the company do next year and the year after? This is the key in determining if the company is a buy or a sell. However, it is the price-earnings ratio that indicates the best time to buy or sell. Simple extrapolations from current earnings figures are useful guides and are probably as accurate as most sophisticated models. Investors are willing to pay considerable sums for what they regard as superior information on company prospects. Witness the plethora of market letters and other financial information services, some indeed superior. However, a number of academic studies have questioned the ability of predictors to predict earnings. Changes in earnings apparently follow a random path, successive changes being statistically independent from what has gone before. Earnings patterns, in brief, have low predictive value. Even so, for most market participants, they are the only act in town. Fundamental analysis would be very thin soup if no projections of corporate earnings were made or attempted.

The price-earnings ratio has the simple virtue of indicating whether a company's shares are overpriced or underpriced. There are a number of ways of judging: as measured against market averages, against the industry's average and against the highs and lows of the company's own past averages. If the Dow Jones Industrial Average is selling with a price-earnings ratio of 12, the company with a price-earnings ratio of 8 may well be underpriced compared with the market. But if that industry rarely sells at a price-earnings above 5, the company is probably overpriced, and it's drastically overpriced if over the last five years the average price earnings high was 6 and the low, 3. The price-earnings ratio does not indicate what a company is worth but rather relative value.

In the quest to determine what a company is worth, security analysts and money managers frequently use the company's book value as a guide. By subtracting the total liabilities from the total assets and then dividing that number—the net assets—by the number of shares outstanding, one arrives at the book value, or stockholder's equity per share. (Any senior equity such as preferred shares must be deducted from the net assets before calculating the book value.)

Book value has of late become fashionable again. During the long drought and depression in the securities markets in the 1970s, shareholder's equity was not a persuasive analytical tool. Too many companies were selling at about or below their book value. However, in boom times and bull markets, investors scan lists of securities selling below book value. As with so many market indicators, book value can be a two-edged sword; a company whose current price is significantly below its shareholders' equity may conceal substantial value just waiting for the investing public to appreciate it and bid it up. On the other hand, the low price may reflect serious trouble within a company.

The first step is to separate the wheat from the chaff by referring to the general indexes. If the Dow Jones Industrials or the Standard & Poor's are selling at or below book value, then the averages will have a lot of company. If the averages are selling at 50 percent to 65 percent above book value, then companies selling dramatically below book are more likely to be disaster areas than not.

With a little manipulation of the balance sheet, the concept of book value can be refined for more critical use. The problem is how to raise or make visible those hidden values if they do indeed exist. This can be done only by examining the quality of the assets. To arrive at net assets, total liabilities are subtracted from total assets. However, long-term assets can be illusory and sometimes deceptive; it is difficult to assess the real values of plant, real estate and equipment. Are they held at cost or replacement value? Should the company fail, would they really be worth what is stated on the balance sheet or would the breakup value be much less? Since there are no easy answers to these questions, why not just look at the quick assets—what remains after subtracting all the liabilities from the current assets. Quick assets per share is then a useful guide to how much the company is worth in ready cash. Some companies do not have a positive quick asset value due to their financial structure, especially finance, insurance and transportation companies, which show negative quick assets.

A look at a list of companies with positive quick assets will reveal that their market prices usually exceed their quick assets per share. However, the real value exists in companies where the market price of their shares is less than that of their quick assets. These companies are selling at substantial discounts from their ready cash, without even considering the value of their long-term assets, which may be considerable. When discovered, either as merger and acquisition targets or as sharply depressed value, such companies do very well in bull markets.

To many market participants, looking for undervalued securities is a bit too much like bottom fishing. Value can be revealed in a more aggressive fashion, especially with the aid of the computer. The computer, with its number-crunching ability, does not innovate as much as it facilitates the discovery of value. Institutions and individuals, not to mention commercial computer programs sold over the counter, have established a series of basic yardsticks. If a given security passes through the screen of half a dozen or a dozen criteria, it becomes a candidate to buy. (Systems designed to sell short have received a lot less attention.) Obviously, the criteria are all important since they can be arranged to include or exclude cyclical companies and growth or defense issues. Some of the more popular tests evaluate the following fundamentals:

- Price-earnings ratio
- Return on equity
- Revenue growth rate
- Earnings growth rate
- Debt/equity ratio
- Dividend yield
- Beta coefficient (volatility)
- Working capital (current assets over current liabilities)
- Book value
- Profit margin

With these measurements in place, it is possible for an investor to choose a security that meets the prescribed standards. For example, a company should have a profit margin of 7 percent; present price not to exceed book value by more than twice; current assets to exceed current liabilities by two but no more than three times; a beta coefficient (a measurement of volatility) of 2; a dividend between 5 percent and 7 percent; debt not to exceed more than 25 percent of equity; earnings growth of no less than 10 percent; revenue growth of no less than 5 percent; return on equity of no less than 7 percent; price-earnings ratio of no more than 8. Such a model, or some variation thereof, will keep an investor out of trouble if applied consistently and with discipline.

Still, there are two problems with this method. First, it lacks sex appeal, so to speak. The system is well calculated to keep one out of new, developmental companies until they have a "respectable" track record. This indeed may be wise if preservation of capital is a top priority. But this "foolproof" formula would have kept prospective investors away from the early stages of Polaroid, Xerox, Syntex, MCI, Apple, and any number of high-tech stocks.

Which leads us to the second problem. Analyzing the financials is apt to place too much credibility on numbers and not enough on intangibles that are less easily measured, such as management techniques. Does the company have an entrepreneurial spirit? How much does it spend on research and development as a percentage of sales, and does that show growth each year? Are there new products in the pipeline? How old is senior management and when did it last change? How are labor-management relations? Are there profit-sharing arrangements or other worker incentives?

There are, in brief, a variety of important aspects of a corporation that determine whether it is a superior or inferior investment but that cannot easily be reduced to numbers. Nevertheless, that information is, according to some observers, already built into the market price. And since some of these factors are not quantifiable, why not simply study the price action and forget about information that is incomplete at best? Enter the technicians.

The Technicians

True market technicians are completely indifferent to fundamental analysis; to them, what a corporation does for a living, the economic environment, fiscal policies and political considerations are of mere academic interest. While not denying the validity of fundamental analysis, technicians are concerned solely with the price action of a market or security, especially with the forces of supply and demand that affect price. You can tell technicians by their slogans: "Don't fight the tape," "The tape tells all," "The trend is your friend" and the like. In brief, fundamental factors are believed accounted for in the current market price.

Technicians have developed a large and influential following in recent years, due in part to some real contributions they have made to understanding market timing and in part, ironically, to publicity given them by academic economists attempting to undermine the validity of their methods.

The technical approach is not a Johnny-come-lately. Some of the elements originated almost a hundred years ago in editorials by Charles Dow, a founder of the *Wall Street Journal*. The Dow Theory, as it became known, was refined by Dow's associate William P. Hamilton and by Robert Rhea. Both Hamilton and Rhea wrote books in the early 1930s developing this market barometer and legitimating its existence, but the present Dow Jones & Company disavows any connection to the theory or the legion of its forecasters.

The Dow Theory was not conceived as a guide to stock prices but was a measure of the nation's business activity as reflected by the stock market. According to the theory, the market is composed of three trends: "the tide," a major trend that constitutes a bull or bear market; "the waves," an intermediate movement confirming or negating the price trend; and "the ripples," patternless day-to-day fluctuations.

The Dow's claim to fame is that it purports to foretell changes in the primary market trend. If the Dow Jones Industrials and the Transportation (previously the Rails) keep making new highs (or lows) in lockstep, the trend remains intact. Since the first index can be read as a reflection of productive capacity and the second as a reflection of the volume of goods being shipped, as long as they both rise (or fall), the economy will maintain its momentum. When they go in different directions, a reversal of economic activity, and consequently of market price, is in the offing. The problem for Dow theorists is to tell the difference between a change in the primary trend (the tide) and a change in the secondary trend (the waves). To separate the true signal from the false, Dow theorists measure the height or depth of the indexes. As long as the crests are higher than those preceding them, and the troughs higher than previous troughs, the trend is intact and the tide clearly bullish. When the tide is turning, both the crest and trough of the next wave will be lower—a signal to sell. If only one of the indexes doesn't confirm, or if the crest or trough acts in opposite fashion, the signal is ambiguous. In a bear market, the theory applies in reverse: The tide doesn't turn bullish until each rally is higher than the previous one and each setback is also higher.

Over the years, the Dow Theory has been analyzed and refined. Volume and configurations are used to interpret the ambiguous messages. Certain configurations are especially meaningful signals, such as "double tops," when averages climb to a certain point, fall off and climb back to the same level, only to fall off once more. The double top is a symptom that the bull market is about to reverse itself. In a bear market, the reversal configuration is a "double bottom." Volume studies suggest that if the indexes break the upward or downward channel on high volume, then the move is valid, but on low volume it is not. Or, to put it another way, decreasing volume on declines is bullish, while increasing volume on declines is bearish. Volume confirms trends.

It is this presumption of trends that has drawn so much criticism of technicians. Dow theorists have been criticized before on several counts: The confirmed warnings of major reversals are frequently late; the signals are far from clear, with no simple way to distinguish between a technical readjustment and a major reversal; and finally, there is no guarantee that the Dow's 30 Industrials and 20 Transportation stocks represent the whole market. But the major criticism has been with the whole idea that a pattern of past prices has any predictive value.

The idea that security prices move randomly was first suggested by a Frenchman at the turn of the century. The analogy was made that one can no more tell where a drunk in a field will wander than tell where subsequent daily prices for a company's shares will move. This random walk theory—in recent years given modern formulation at the University of Chicago's Center for Research in Security Prices—was based on one very simple assumption: In the marketplace, prices are continually being adjusted to reflect all relevant information. Stock prices are based on the accumulation of many bits of randomly generated noise: the public facts and forecasts upon which participants act. Given an efficient market, where buyers and sellers compete for profit and have access to all pertinent news, prices at any given time would reflect a share's intrinsic worth. But since the opinions of traders and investors differ, prices tend to fluctuate around the intrinsic worth. Were these fluctuations uniform or consistent, one could trade profitably. However, there is no consistency since competition neutralizes various opinions and prices continue to wander randomly about the consensus value. The consensus will change with each new piece of relevant information, but the changes are not connected in a series, and therefore price changes have little predictive value in an efficient market.

In other words, if the market is as efficient as proponents of the random walk theory suggest, not only is additional analysis of stocks useless, but there are no knowable trends. This conclusion is a frontal attack on technical analysis—and to some degree on common sense. If professional money managers do no better than monkeys throwing darts at stock lists, who needs them? If one can perform only in an average way, assuming average risk-reward odds, then there is no need for an elaborate financial community tendering advice and no need to achieve more than the mediocre. The Center for Research in Security Prices defined the mediocre—the average rate of return from 56,577,538 hypothetical combinations of buying and selling 1,715 common stocks listed on the New York Stock Exchange over a 35-year period (1926–60). It was a little better than 9 percent per annum. More recent studies confirm this long-term rate of return. But there are certain periods which have exceeded that return: The rate for the decade 1982 to 1992 was over 17 percent.

The random walk and the efficient market hypotheses were provocative but not helpful in investing money, nor were they necessarily accurate representations of market behavior. Certainly no prudent person would invest by throwing darts even if he had a marginal chance of doing better than the average. Some professional money managers do no better than average and some do worse, but there are also some who consistently do better than the market. Obviously, the results of the latter group are not random. Their success, as is true of all investors who consistently improve on the median, is attributable either to the inefficiencies of the market or to the investor's willingness to take on a ratio of risk with which the average investor would not be willing to live.

Market efficiency is uneven at best. At times investors become overly pessimistic and the price-earnings ratio of the averages plummets; at other times they are overly optimistic and the price-earnings ratio skyrockets. The reduction in interest rates and the perception that there would be light at the end of the recession's tunnel in 1982 was enough to buoy prices. Was the market efficient at 780 on the Dow Jones Industrial Average and inefficient at 1,240 six months later, vice versa, both, or neither? Or take the case of the great market crash in 1987: in August the Dow reached a high of 2,722, but on October 20th the Dow index fell to 1739, a drop of 36 percent. At which point was the market efficient, and at which point not?

There is, of course, no sure way of telling, but it is obvious that while there is much truth to the cliché that a security is worth only what someone is willing to pay for it, there are times when securities are dramatically overpriced or dramatically underpriced.

Inefficiencies are even more manifest in the pricing of some companies. Neglect, size and type of industry are all factors that can contribute to low multiples. The 60 largest brokerage houses and investment banks monitor the top 2,500 companies. Since there are close to 40,000 public corporations, a large number are either not covered or only superficially covered. The ones that are not analyzed, the ones that have no institutional investors, are probably inefficiently priced—and they are probably undervalued, too. Companies that are under everyone's microscope are probably efficiently priced and fully valued, and no amount of security analysis by a private investor is likely to yield any new information or insight.

Periods of inflation also cause inefficient pricing, as witnessed during the 1970s. Even though it was gospel that stocks do well during inflationary times, that period was certainly the exception to the rule. In fact, even when adjusted for inflation, Standard & Poor's 400 stock index shrunk by 38 percent. What was supposed to make stocks a good inflation hedge was the presumption that companies could raise prices faster than wages, which in turn would increase profits. In the 1960s, when inflation was still relatively mild, this view prevailed. But as inflation picked up and interest rates also rose, the negative side of inflation became more apparent. Inventory profits might prove to be illusory; plant and equipment were underdepreciated so that down the road, replacements would cost far more; and the government was overtaxing doubtful corporate earnings. The result was depressed equity prices, except perhaps for companies rich in natural resources. The public's perception of inflation—at one point benevolent, at another malevolent—caused great inefficiencies in the marketplace, which shrewd investors and acquisition-oriented companies were quick to take advantage of.

In 1994 and 1995 the Federal Reserve's Alan Greenspan saw inflation around the corner and proceeded to ratchet up short-term interest rates. While bond prices took a header, stock prices rose, no doubt caused by better corporate earnings, but perhaps to some degree by the perception of higher commodity and consumer prices.

Charting

Technical analysts presume that there are trends and cycles, and naturally they have no faith in random walks based on efficient market pricing. By studying volume and chart configurations, one can obtain clues to a pattern. Other clues come from data generated by market activity. Indicators such as advance/decline ratios, insider trading, market momentum indexes, put and call ratios, short sale ratios and other special or proprietary indicators help technicians discover the meaning of the market's behavior. It should be noted that there are fierce debates among the cognoscenti and gurus who use these yardsticks about their value and what precisely they show. For the uninitiated, technical analysis can be confusing unless handled very judiciously and sparingly.

Charting is the basic tool of technicians, a technique developed more than a hundred years ago. There are two kinds of charts: the vertical line, or bar, chart and the point and figure chart. Although both tell the same story, their preparation is different. Bar charts are simple graphic representations of daily (or sometimes weekly or monthly) stock prices—their highs, lows and closing prices. An entry on graph paper is made every trading day, and volume bars are maintained at the bottom.

Point and figure charting is more complicated (some say purer) since it lacks the dimension of time. On chart paper, x's, o's or actual prices are entered if there is a substantial and predetermined change or reversal from the previous price. Prices are plotted vertically, usually in half-point, one-point or two-point gradations, until there is a change in trend, when the next vertical column is started. There is no volume measurement.

Both types of charts are meant to identify the five phases that constitute a cycle in the life of a stock movement. They are: (1) accumulation; (2) recovery; (3) speculation; (4) distribution; and (5) readjustment. In the accumulation stage prices fluctuate narrowly, producing a horizontal trendline. This accumulation or congestion is ended when a "breakout" occurs. In an upside penetration, buyers are willing to pay increasingly higher prices for stock, and in a downside penetration, sellers are willing to accept decreasingly lower prices to be out of the stock. Often this disequilibrium and breakout constitute a recovery phase for purchasers who bought at higher levels. As prices go higher speculators jump aboard, accentuating the trend. When prices reach a new plateau and no more new speculators or traders join in, a period of distribution unfolds, as profit takers sell their stock. Prices then readjust downward as they penetrate the downside trendline.

In theory, these five basic phases have distinct configurations, but in reality they are often hard to discern. For instance, a classic head and shoulders formation is a pictograph of speculation, distribution and readjustment; a double bottom can be interpreted as accumulation and recovery stages. There are coils, rounding bottoms, inverted triangles, saucers, gaps and other shapes, but, needless to say, patterns are more easily identified in hindsight. Interpreting charts is an arcane science, but charts do give an investor a bird's-eye view of a security's price history.

There are some recurrent trading patterns for chart watchers to bear in mind. The trendline, or trading channel, gives an idea of the immediate price range; all other things being equal, it is cheaper to buy when the price is in the lower sector and more profitable to sell when it is in the upper sector of the channel. The upper and lower trendlines indicate resistance and support levels, critical areas for technicians. If the price penetrates either one on substantial volume, it is a clue to buy or sell the shares. The appearance of a violation of a trading channel is one of the most significant clues for market analysts, for it signifies immediate action. Even fundamentalists take this behavior into account before trading.

Besides charts, technicians use other indicators, as noted earlier, to measure the internal strength of the market. There are dozens of different figures (some of dubious value), but the following ones (in no specific order) are those that receive the most attention and bear watching.

Volume figures have been refined, largely due to the work of Joseph E. Granville, who introduced the concept of "on balance volume." Volume figures for a stock (or the general market) are ignored if there is no price change, but for up days Granville defined trading as demand volume, on down days as supply volume. By netting out the difference, one can see whether supply or demand is stronger at the end of a series of days or weeks, even if the price remains unchanged at the end of the sequence. Stock can be up one point the first day on 10,000 shares, down one-half point the second day on 5,000 shares, down one point the third day on 10,000 shares, up one point the fourth day on 15,000 shares and down one-half point the fifth day on 5,000 shares. At the end of the week, the price has remained the same but the on-balance volume indicates that there was demand volume (+5,000) for shares, a bullish sign since buying is stronger than selling. Technical financial services have different formulas for figuring on-balance volume, or uptick and downtick strength, but the object is to reveal whether buying or selling strength prevails regardless of price movement. Obviously, price changes confirm the conclusion.

Another widely used indicator is the "moving average." Its purpose is to smooth out erratic price movements of an especially volatile issue. This is accomplished by simply adding up all the closing prices of the previous days (or weeks)—10 days, 30 days or 200 days (or 10 weeks or 30 weeks)—and dividing by the number of days (or weeks) in the series. On the following day, the first day is dropped and the new day added. If the price of the stock rises above the moving average, this is a positive sign; conversely, if it falls below the moving average, it is bearish. To put it another way, a change in the trend is in the offing if the moving average stops rising and begins to turn down, or vice versa. The trend reversal, so proponents claim, becomes clearer from the early warning signal of the moving average. The signal can be refined by calculating the average's deviation—by dividing the final stock price in the sequence by the moving average. When plotted on a horizontal axis in conjunction with the moving average, the average deviation is another early warning if the price of the shares is prematurely out of line, either overbought or oversold. Most of the financial chart services plot moving averages but not the average deviation.

Another indicator of market stamina is the "advance/decline ratio," the number of shares on either of the two major exchanges that reflect the breadth of a movement. Stock indexes, especially the narrowly based Dow Jones Industrials, can be moving ahead, but the underlying strength can be in jeopardy if it is not accompanied by broad market participation. A negative advance/decline ratio with a rising market is a sign of imminent trouble.

Short sales are considered to be especially meaningful since so few investors understand the technique of selling what they do not own. Therefore, two groups of short sellers have acquired reputations as bellwethers: one because it is presumed always to be wrong, the other for the opposite reason. In the first case, "odd lot short sales ratio" are sales made by traders who sell fewer than 100 shares. The word on Wall Street is that they are far more often wrong than right. If you divide odd lot short sales by total odd lot sales (or, as an alternative, an average of odd lot purchases and sales), the resulting ratio will indicate if the market is on negative or positive ground. On average, the ratio has hovered at 1.25 percent. If the ratio is 3 percent to 5 percent—meaning that an unusually large number of odd lotters are selling—the market is ready for an advance. (Parenthetically, the higher the short interest, the greater the demand for stock to cover positions—an added fillip to the market.) When the ratio declines to 0.5 percent—meaning that few odd lotters are selling—the market is poised for a reversal or correction. Odd lotters have generally had a bum rap, and their market performance at times has been quite apropos. But in market extremes they have tended to panic. Hence their value as an indicator.

The second short sale guide is the "New York Stock Exchange member short sales ratio." Who knows better than the brokers themselves that "no tree grows to the sky"? Member sentiment can be gauged by dividing member short sales by total short sales: If the figure is over 80 percent, the prospects are for a falling market; under 60 percent, members expect a rally. A more limited indicator can be calculated by specialists' shorts, but since shorting is an integral part of providing liquidity in making the market, the ratio is somewhat hedged and less meaningful than member short sales.

Of increasing popularity as an indicator are "insider trading" statistics, which reflect the transactions of officers and directors of a company or of any investors (or other corporations) who control more than 5 percent of the company. Such insiders are obliged to report their dealings in company shares to the Securities and Exchange Commission, and they are subsequently published. Are insiders better traders? Do they show superior performance? It depends. On the buy side, insiders appreciate when their company is dramatically underpriced, but on the sell side, their actions are a less reliable guide. Although insiders will sell stock when the shares are fully priced (when the market price has finally caught up with the shares' true value), they will also sell for reasons that have nothing to do with the market, from paying school tuition to buying real estate.

Other indicators abound: liquidity or cash on hand of investment companies and pension funds; margin debt of stock exchange customers; money supply figures; and seasonal, cyclical, psychological and political measurements that may or may not have predictive value. Dyed-in-the-wool technicians have their own pet indicators, from the hemline index to esoteric wave theories of a long-dead Russian economist. Perhaps the one thing that unites all of these observers is their continuing, endless search for a theory or a collection of indicators that will not only explain past market performance but also predict future supply and demand forces for the market and a company's shares.

CHAPTER 10

Investing by the Numbers

News known is news discounted.

—Anonymous

Computers, Databases and Programs

The phrases "programmed buying" and "programmed selling" are now heard throughout the land. A brief ten years ago they were virtually unknown; today, no student of the market can afford not to grasp their meaning. In brief, they are securities transactions that are triggered by a formula, and increasingly the formula is the work of the eighth wonder of the world—the computer.

The computer's role in personal finance was bound to grow as the price of computer hardware dropped. By the early 1990s, personal computers with list prices of $1,500 had the computational power of machines that cost $500,000 in the mid-1970s. The price fall in hardware was soon followed by an explosion in communication devices and networks that enable electronic terminals—be they teletype machines, dumb terminals, intelligent typewriters, word processors or even video game machine keyboards—to communicate with mainframe hardware. Through a series of long-distance telephonic networks, such as SprintNet, AutoNet, Uninet, Datapac in Canada and the most ubiquitous one, Internet, these terminals can talk to massive computer libraries and databases nationally and even internationally. All that's needed is a coupling device called a modem; the terminal can send its digital electronic pulse over ordinary telephone lines to query a database, and the immediate response is either printed on paper or appears on a cathode ray tube (CRT) or television monitor.

At first, these electronic libraries were primarily for professionals in medicine, law, engineering and journalism. Accessing databases was expensive ($1 or $2 per minute of connect time), and instructions and programs—written by and for the experts—were not always "user friendly." But as happens with most commodities, the price of information came down and ease of access increased. And a number of services were started for consumers and investors.

Computer-generated information is not new to the investment world. Indeed, since the 1960s a number of financial institutions have used computers to store information and develop investment programs. Trend analysis was one of the first serious undertakings of the early pioneers. The work was complicated and expensive. There was no ready-made library of machine-readable information, let alone software. The democratization of electronic information and data processing—"a terminal in every pot, a newswire in every garage," according to one observer—was still more than a decade off.

With the advent of the microprocessor and the personal computer, all that changed. Business information is now collected, collated and correlated by dozens of publishers, databases, financial service organizations and news agencies. An abundance of information is available at a reasonable price. Market participants can research every aspect of economic and business conditions that affect corporate affairs and stock prices, from the latest company news to obscure SEC filings. A brief review of some of the major sources of computer-generated information follows, in no special order:

Dow Jones & Company—the publisher of the *Wall Street Journal, Barron's,* and the Dow Jones news service, popularly known as the broad tape—provides a variety of dial-up services through its News/Retrieval service. Most of the information originates within Dow Jones, and its menu of databases is extensive, including News, Current Quotes, Historical Quotes, Sports, Weather and Movie Reviews. It offers a Free Text Search, which enables a subscriber to find information and manipulate it to fit specific questions, from all Dow Jones publications dating back to mid-1979. In addition, News/Retrieval carries some databases that are prepared by other organizations: a Corporate Earnings Estimator for 2,400 widely followed companies; Disclosure, a service that abstracts information on 6,000 public companies on file with the SEC; Media General Financial Services, analyses of companies and industry groups broken down by price and volume data and fundamental data; Academic American Encyclopedia, which presents general background information; Wall Street Week, a full-text transcript of the popular television show; and Weekly Economic Services, a survey of economic trends.

Mead Data Central developed a broad-based information system called Nexis, which was recently sold to the Dutch publisher Elsevier. Though not strictly a financial service organization, the Nexis data bank holds full-text articles from many of the major business and financial publications throughout the world as well as from general publications. Nexis also has access to the *Encylopaedia Britannica* and the Federal Register. This interactive database was enhanced by the acquisition of the New York Times Information Service. The Times Information Bank holds abstracts from the *New York Times*, going back to 1969, and from five dozen other newspapers, magazines and journals. In brief, the combination of both services offers subscribers a massive amount of current information.

There are now three major on-line services—Prodigy, Compuserve and America Online—plus a host of smaller, more specialized interactive services. A prodigious amount of information is generated by these services, and all have special business and financial databases that customers can access: current (delayed 15 minutes) stock quotations, historical quotes, business stories, company profiles and graphic charts, plus the news services from the major wire agencies. A subscriber can be kept as abreast of the markets as any professional.

Though relatively new, these database retrieval systems already have tens of thousands of sophisticated subscribers; their rates are geared for the consumer market. There are other computer-generated financial services geared for professionals, which are more expensive: Standard & Poor's Compustat Service, Inc., Telescan, Signal, Dial Data, and BMI are the more popular ones, while Bloomberg, Bridge, Knight-Rider and Telerate are used mostly by institutions. Still other databases—Predicast and Dialog, for instance—provide extensive and exhaustive information on commerce and business forecasting. Clients may subscribe to one service or to a group of different bases from a middleman distributor or vendor.

Internet, the worldwide computer network, is revolutionizing database searches. New sources of information are made available daily, either free or for a nominal charge. Computer users can now access this vast collection of sources through the World Wide Web and any of its search engines. One can call up company home pages for the latest financial information, or the SEC's EDGAR (electronic data gathering, analysis and retrieval) for the latest filings. Other government agencies have their own bulletin boards, such as the Department of Commerce, Labor Statistics, Census and the Treasury. Even the Federal Reserve System is now providing current statistics on Treasury auctions, and surveys of business activity. One of the hottest electronic links for financial information is Onramp Access's Stocks and Commodities page of Internet Interactive Marketing out of Austin, Texas. This site has an extensive menu: QuoteCom, a market data and wire service, and connections with university-provided research papers from Washington University, University of Michigan, MIT and NYU, among others. Still other Web sites provide summaries of stock recommendations from major brokerage houses (Recommendations Update), and quote services (PC Stock Quote Service, Security APL Quote Server, Networth Equities Center). And finally, not to be left out in the dash for digital destiny, are the brokerage houses with their own home pages providing research abstracts and recommendations: J. P. Morgan & Co., Aufhauser & Co., Gruntal & Co. and Wertheim Schroder & Co. No doubt much of this information is repetitive, and some is probably irrelevant for market purposes, but there is now a surfeit compared with the short supply a decade ago.

No two consumers of these interactive systems use them in quite the same fashion, any more than two readers of a newspaper or magazine come away with the same understanding, knowledge or course of action. What these services can do is reduce the amount of research effort that goes into portfolio management while extending the scope of that research. For example, say you wish to check out a tip or learn more about the new field of genetic engineering, with a view toward selecting some companies that are on the cutting edge of developments. You also have certain financial requirements that securities must meet before you purchase them for your portfolio. Through one or a combination of these retrieval services, you can find all the recent major stories on bioengineering and genetic recombinant technology in the leading business journals. From your reading, you can compile a list of the companies that generate the most interest. By searching news banks you can then get the most current information. Through a financial database, you can obtain all the fundamental corporate background, and through a library of prices you can have access to trends and technical price action. By checking the disclosure documents of the SEC, you note whether there are any problems or insider trading or other activity. You can find enough corporate information to see if the company meets your own investment criteria, such as profit margins, return on investment, equity/debt ratios, and so on. Finally, you can gain access to a financial database that projects earnings based on the published reports of Wall Street analysts. You have "interfaced" for an hour or two with data banks, from your home or office, spent $50 or $100 in connect charges, and gathered as much current information on the topic and the companies as is possible and pertinent. Such a search before the creation of electronic libraries would have taken days of frustrating research work—if one could even have found all the right documents. Now, for a relatively low cost, you can mount a full-scale investigation; you are far better informed and have no doubt markedly improved your chances for investment success.

Calculating Computers

A growing number of investors have taken computers and computer-generated information services a step further. Not content with raw information, they have either compiled their own software programs or purchased one or more of the growing number of software systems prepared by commercial programming companies. These programs manipulate information in a variety of ways and ultimately provide guides to action. No program yet promises to "beat the market," though they all imply that they might do just that, but they can reduce some of the tedium and labor for the investor.

There are more than a hundred commercial software systems dedicated to improving market performance. For the most part, they are published on floppy discs, 3.5-inch magnetic plastic sheets with electronic instructions that, when placed on the disc drive or hard drive, prepare the computer for a specific format.

Investing by computer may well be the wave of the future, but for the foreseeable future it will not be easy or inexpensive. Unlike data banks, which require little more than a single keyboard terminal and modem, computer programs require a CPU—a central processing unit, the brain of a computer, with communications capability. In addition, one needs a disc drive, a CRT or TV monitor and/or a printer, and a modem. The hardware, regardless of which of the hundred computers one chooses, is likely to exceed a couple of thousand dollars.

The software can be almost as expensive as the hardware. Programs can range from $150 for the simplest to $3,600 for highly sophisticated analytical tools. Many of the programs are based on some form of technical analysis, but the most straightforward ones are fundamental and rely on classic security analysis.

Since there are many different approaches, it is not possible to give a full explanation of all the programs available. But an idea of this brave new world can be gathered from some general programs. First, there are very basic programs, which are not much more than accounting packages for maintaining portfolios. These programs can be useful in caring for complicated positions: portfolios with a mix of stocks, bonds, options, municipals, commercial paper, Treasury paper and mutual funds. And these systems are useful for maintaining multiple accounts. By manipulating securities information against portfolio position information, these programs can quickly present a portfolio appraisal: inventory of shares, current price, current market value, interest or dividend rate, annual income, yield, percent of type security or total of portfolio. With a day-end update, these systems can reveal unrealized capital gains and losses, both long- and short-term. They will also keep a record of realized capital gains and losses. For those maintaining multiple accounts, these programs will also cross-reference all securities to show who owns what.

Some of the more popular basic systems are offered through accounting and bookkeeping packages, as well as tax preparation software. These bookkeeping programs are valuable to anyone who manages portfolios, for with just a few keystrokes the program will update all prices and transactions. But they offer no guidance. Guidance can be offered by fundamental programs, but such guidance is based on the criteria that the investor chooses to use. It is up to the user to pick which of the dozens of fundamental programs are relevant for the stock and bond selection process and to build his own system on top of the program's capabilities. Some of the information is from the balance sheet, some from the income statement, and some from the flow of funds. An investor wishes to know such critical information as profit margins, return on investment, percent change of earnings for the last quarter and last year, debt/equity ratio, book value, price-earnings ratio, current ratio and dividend yield. Once he has the information, he has to put it to use.

Let's say the investor is interested only in companies that have a profit margin greater than 10 percent, a return on equity of more than 15 percent and a revenue growth of 10 percent per year, that are selling at a discount from book value, have a current price-earnings ratio of less than 8, have a current ratio of assets to liabilities of no less than 2.5 to 1 and have a dividend yield of at least 7 percent. First he draws up a list of stocks or industries he wishes to follow. The most recent information is gathered from one of the major computer databases and downloaded into his personal computer or microprocessor for manipulation. A list of the stocks that meet his criteria will appear on his computer monitor or printout. Some programs will also warn of price alerts.

Whether or not an investor can perform successful fundamental market analysis on his personal computer depends largely on his own prerogatives and prejudices—and on his ability to interpret what he learns. The system's great virtue, perhaps, is that it holds one's feet to the fire by providing a consistent formula that must be followed.

Technical Analysis

Software for technical analysis is more common than the fundamental kind. It, too, calls upon dial-up financial data banks for current information about price and volume. Depending on which program is under consideration, it organizes the information to conform with the specific theory. Some of these theories are extraordinarily complicated, such as the Gann's Square of Nine program, which tries to identify "potential market reversal points . . . with multi-axis overlays to generate a predictive histogram." Whew!

Others are relatively simple. The most common ones produce line and bar charts for price and volume action, whether for T-bills, commodities or common stock. These graphs go back 30 days or 9 months, showing highs, lows and moving averages. Other programs give more sophisticated information, such as arbitrage analysis for various monetary instruments, yield spreads and yield curve analysis—all of which offer clues to present trading opportunities. Some of these systems require updating by the user; others require no user input (discs are sent periodically). Some even operate automatically on a household appliance timer; quotes are obtained and analysis is performed each evening for review the next morning.

An old tool for technicians is the point and figure chart. Unlike bar graphs, which incorporate price range, trading volume and periodic time values, point and figure charting is based solely on price. Alternating columns of x's and o's for fixed price increments are used to produce a pattern. Since prices never move in one direction only, a column of x's is used to trace increasing prices and a column of o's traces decreasing prices. After a direction has been determined and charted, the only important question is what constitutes a reversal of a price trend. Most chartists use three points, each point representing $1. Only when the price has fallen or risen more than three points from the column's low or high is a reversal identified. The accumulation of ascending and descending columns makes a well-defined pattern as the price bounces back and forth between resistance and support levels. By recognizing these patterns or congestion areas, the investor can take advantage of subsequent moves and breakouts.

When point and figure charting is done with a computer, the parameters can easily be changed, the configurations altered or extended and display capabilities enhanced. Computerization gives easy updates and can produce graphs quickly on any number of charts.

Many software programs are dedicated to analyzing volume as a means of understanding market action. Simple price and volume changes tend to confirm each other; the real problem for technicians is to explain what is happening when the two diverge. If there is more supply than demand, the outlook is pessimistic. If more demand than suppy, the outlook is optimistic. Thus, by analyzing net cumulative volume, one can confirm or anticipate price trends. Computer graphics can superimpose the two curves and divergences are available for visual analysis.

Other software programs are based on very sophisticated math or engineering theories: Regression Analysis, Relative Strength Index, Fourier Analysis, Momentum Index and Stochastic Process, to name a few. These various systems are used, domestically and worldwide, for stock, bonds, commodities, options and futures. While there are reports of improved performance, no single system seems to work all the time. As yet, no one "owns the exchange," nor is that a possibility, for interpretation is still a highly individual matter. Investors, traders and speculators will view levels of risk and reward quite differently and will act in contrary fashion on the same given information.

The most recent trend in computer software are neural networks. These software packages try to emulate thought patterns, simulating brain waves and massaging given data. The object is to replicate superior performance from past successful patterns. Whether this form of artificial intelligence works remains to be seen.

Computerized investing makes for less drudgery in keeping and posting records, but it also makes the investor work harder at keeping abreast of the abundance of new information. There is a very real danger that all this computer-generated information will overwhelm the user if it is not carefully structured. A selective, personalized program can both enhance the possibilities of profit and eliminate from consideration the mounting mass of irrelevant materials. While "programmed buying" and "programmed selling" have the ring of authority about them, even the most astutely managed funds have fallen victim to the unexpected. A large and prestigious New England money management concern had its computers triggered with buy and sell formulas. One day the computers churned out a large buy order for Braniff Airlines—the very day the company announced it was filing for bankruptcy.

CHAPTER 11

Information and
the Market

*If you buy headlines today, you'll end up selling
newspapers tomorrow.*

—An old market proverb

Business Conditions

Financial markets have changed more in the last decade
than in the entire previous century. There are a number
of separate reasons for this restructuring, but the resulting
change is so massive that it has altered the very nature of
markets and the way people think about them.

The greatest change has been in the huge increase in public participation. Today 51 million direct shareholders (and
uncounted millions of indirect ones) and hundreds of huge
institutions trade tens of millions of shares on a daily basis,
owning 44 percent of the total equity in the country.

Of almost equal importance is the increased professionalization of the investment community. The public now has
a vast array of investment choices, ranging from the basic
services of minimal discount brokers to sophisticated, full-
service financial department stores.

Third, the growing variety of financial instruments now
enables the public to participate in a wide range of opportunities, from high-interest money market funds to highly
leveraged venture capital investments.

But more important than increased participation, professionalization and new opportunities is the growth of that singular phenomenon that makes for successful markets—the free flow of information. Some investors and speculators still act on "hot" tips, purported inside stories and seat-of-the-pants instincts, but increasingly they rely on economic documentation, corporate analysis and technical assessments of market dynamics—in short, on valuable, if not always provable, information.

There has been a veritable information explosion in the financial world; in a generation we have gone from paucity to surfeit. Although we face a genuine danger of having too much information to contend with, that is still preferable to having too little. The problem is how to sort the meaningful from the meaningless, the data one needs to know from that which is only nice to know. There is no simple way to separate the wheat from the chaff, but some trends are visible and noteworthy. The tools for making informed market judgments are available, but it is the responsibility of the investing public to use a critical eye in ferreting out value from a variety of sources.

Information from government agencies is very much a mixed bag. Some of it is important, some of it is presumed to be important and some of it is meaningless or at best confusing. The most consistently important figure, released every Thursday at 4:15 PM, is the measurement of the money supply, M1, by the Federal Reserve System. The importance of the figure is, of course, as an indicator of whether the Fed is letting the money supply increase in a possible attempt to spark inflationary tendencies, holding to a steady course or starving the system for credit in order to rein in a boom or inadvertently dampen a recovery. As one robin doesn't make for spring, one week's aberration in the money supply is not considered important. What is important, according to a number of studies, is a series of unanticipated changes in the money supply that subsequently affect interest rates, especially changes that lie outside the Fed's announced targets. In brief, if the change in M1 agrees with the consensus forecast of the 50 or 60 government securities dealers, the market's reaction will be orderly and predictable. If not, the reaction late Thursday and Friday in the fixed-interest market may be sharp and unexpected and may be a warning that a change in trend is imminent.

The next series of government figures that attracts most media attention are the consumer price index, the GNP, the budget deficit, the unemployment rate, plant capacity utilization, productivity growth, housing starts and automobile production. While none of them evoke an overwhelming market response, they certainly set a tone and are milestones in marking the economy's direction. The public's perception is to regard a rising GNP as good news, but a rising consumer price index as bad; a lower budget deficit as good news, but rising unemployment as bad; rising plant utilization as good, but falling housing starts as bad. These figures, and other government figures of lesser import, wash over the public, leaving no discernible trail in their wake. Professional market observers lend more credence to the series of indicators published in *Business Conditions Digest,* a monthly publication of the Commerce Department that follows 700 business conditions that are divided into three main categories: leading, coincident and lagging.

The leading indicator category, which obviously attracts the most attention, is composed of 11 measurements of the economy that forecast business activity, or at least activity in the industrial sector. The 11, with a base of 1967 = 100, will decline for some months before an actual recession starts and conversely, begin to climb for some months before a recovery. The leading index is composed of manufacturers' new orders, building permits, daily stock prices, inventories of manufactured goods, the layoff rate of factory workers, the average work week for industrial workers, the nation's money supply, net new business start-ups, shipping rates for finished goods, new orders for economic goods, orders for factory equipment and commodity prices. While the leading indicators anticipate the business cycle, the coincident indicators move in lockstep with the business cycle.

The eight coincident indicators are the GNP, personal income, industrial production, manufacturing and trade sales, retail sales, nonagricultural employment and the unemployment rate (inverted). All these tend to rise as the economy recovers.

Finally, the lagging indicators are the number of people unemployed for 15 weeks or more, capital expenses for new plant and equipment, the book value of trade inventories, business loans outstanding and bank rates on short-term loans.

The *Business Conditions Digest* compiles all these key indicators, but they do move erratically at times. No bell is rung when the economy reaches a particular stage or a turning point in the business cycle, but interested observers devise their own formulas or fasten on one or two indicators to tell the whole story. For instance, stock market movements are thought to be revealing, so the S&P 500 Index is watched. But as one wit remarked, the market average has foretold eight out of the last five recessions.

Private Sources

If Washington produces general economic information, the private sector produces specific business news. From newspapers, magazines, journals, newsletters, corporate publicity and public relations, there is more than enough printed material, but in addition investors must now recognize the impact of radio and television broadcasting, electronic data banks and computerized retrieval services. In 1974 a book by two *Wall Street Journal* reporters, Frederick Klein and John Prestbo, looked at the influence of news on the market. They reported that in the course of their investigation, they had found it was safe to eliminate certain media, namely radio and television, from serious consideration, because they didn't deal with business news and when they occasionally did, the coverage was exceedingly superficial. We have come a long way in 20 years and today that observation is no longer true. Radio talk shows find that investment seminars are one of their staples, and cable and direct satellite broadcasts fill the air with a deluge of business news each day. Indeed, in addition to the major commercial networks there is the

CNBC Network, Cable News Network, C-Span, PBS with the Nightly Business Report, Adam Smith and Wall Street Week and the Bloomberg wire. And their impact is direct and immediate. While instant commentary is no substitute for background pieces and more profound analysis, there is no denying that instant communications and the whole gamut of electronic information are having a powerful effect.

Instant or otherwise, the question over the years has been precisely: How does news influence the market? How is information translated into market movements? Is news a leading, lagging or coincident indicator? Not much research has been done on the subject. On the one hand, news seems extraordinarily commonplace and many underlying assumptions are taken for granted. On the other hand, deciphering and applying news reports is a complex process not easily understood, perhaps not even understandable.

News is, of course, the lifeblood of markets, and in the interest of fair and orderly markets news and information are expected to be disseminated quickly. Indeed, it is the law. When the Securities Exchange Act of 1934 was passed, Congress noted that "hiding and secreting of important information obstructs the operations of the markets as indices of real value. There cannot be honest markets without honest publicity." And the Securities and Exchange Commission has added that the "financial community, the accounting profession, and bar and industry generally have come not only to accept, but to support the principle that those who make use of the public's money must supply the information essential to the formulation of intelligent investment decisions."

Nevertheless, all material information is not necessarily released in a timely or orderly fashion, even though it may meet legal and stock exchange requirements. One of the conclusions of the Klein and Prestbo study reinforces what many market observers have long suspected: Companies are likely to be quick to release positive information, be it high quarterly earnings figures or new product information, but slow and hesitant to release negative news. So, although public companies are obliged to make full disclosure of their financial information, they are occasionally tardy, which undoubtedly compounds the damage. Consequently, one rule of thumb for an investor is that the longer it takes a company to come forward with its quarterly operating results or any negative news, the worse the impact is likely to be.

This leads to another point: Most of the news and information published and broadcast by the media is overwhelmingly bullish and optimistic. Perhaps this reflects the American temperament (why so few people sell short), but it is not a true mirror of reality. It is understandable that brokerage houses and investment banks have a vested interest in the public buying shares, and thus only occasionally suggest that shares be sold; presumably this might alienate company sources and jeopardize investment banking relationships. But one should expect more objectivity and critical suspicion from the media. In the face of all the good news it is remarkable that stocks ever decline at all.

Since securities do decline in the face of all the good news, we can assume that the discounting instincts of the public are alive and well, testifying to the fact that Americans don't believe all they hear or read. Just as economists seasonally adjust figures ("Sometimes they adjust the cold out of winter," according to one observer), the public has the healthy ability to interpret and adjust information. Nevertheless, prices tend to move up with overwhelmingly positive news and down with overwhelmingly negative news. Reported Klein and Prestbo, "The news and the market moved in the same direction, indicating that stocks can't continue to fall in the face of a sustained dose of good news, nor continue to rise when the news is decisively bad." In brief, news and information are "concurrent indicators of market movements."

Some analysts would challenge this observation. Sometimes the market seems particularly perverse, and does just the opposite—moving up in the face of bad news and falling in the face of good news. The market has been said to "climb a wall of worry," on occasion.

What is certain is the perception that there is never enough information. Thus investors are forever weighing, evaluating, sifting, absorbing and discarding information to reduce risk in market decisions. But information in itself is no panacea for correct market moves. The paradox with information is that you never know enough for "correct" moves, whether in markets or life in general. No one has stated this problem better than Justin Mamis, a respected technician, in his book *The Nature of Risk*.

> The tape provides insufficient information, even though it is so specific . . . one invariably feels a need, a compulsion, to wait to see one more tick, and then another . . . as if the *next one* will—at last—tell him what he needs to know . . . sort of the way, in the burlesque houses of our youth, we would wait and watch for one more dancer to come out from backstage as if the next dancer would finally reveal the truth. What *is* known—the previous tick, the one now known—is never enough.

Good News/Bad News

In trying to understand how the market digests information, it is necessary to separate good news from bad news. The problem, however, is that some news is thought to be positive by some investors and negative by others. Naturally, disagreements are what make the markets interesting—if disconcerting. Even the simplest hypothesis can be translated in contradictory fashion. For example, on the face of it, drought and subsequent starvation are ecological and human disasters, but commodity food prices will jump in the face of shortages, causing joy in the hearts of farmers and processors. Conversely, huge harvests will send prices crashing as producers compete to unload, causing havoc and foreclosures in the farm belt. Perhaps the final irony is that consumers in the drought area may starve (unless there is global intervention), not because there is a lack of edible grains elsewhere, but because of the cost of transportation and the lack of a delivery infrastructure. In a famine everyone—consumers, farmers, distributors, processors, hedgers, speculators—has a different interest to protect and each group acts accordingly, often at cross purposes.

War, of course, is the ultimate social catastrophe, but again, the markets act variously in response to war news. In themselves, markets are not capitalist institutions, but free markets certainly augment the process of free enterprise. Since wars tend to restrict markets and the free flow of goods, it might be presumed that war is detrimental to capital formation. Yet Marxists and socialists have long argued the opposite, that capitalism and the profit system feed on wars, that war economies are the "cure" for depressed and inefficient systems.

Thus two schools of thought are at odds as to how markets react when faced with war news and actual hostilities. One group maintains that defense and military procurement will play a prominent role in economic planning so the sectors involved in defense will assuredly benefit. Ergo, war is bullish for stocks. The other school contends that military spending is extraordinarily wasteful since it produces no useful consumer goods and, more important, that all that spending for nonusable hardware creates inflation, which destroys the value of currency. Moreover, war taxes and the loss of consumer markets make war unprofitable. In their view, it is a cessation of hostilities and an end to war scares that are bullish.

The most recent conflict, the Gulf War, provides an illustration of market moves and war. Whether or not the market knew anything of Saddam Hussein's intentions, it had been topping out for a year before the actual Kuwait invasion on August 2, 1990. By that time the market was 200 Dow points lower. Imminent war was not good for stocks. However, as soon as Desert Storm commenced the market rallied, convinced that the war would be short and devastating. Which it was!

There seems to be some truth in both schools. In the 20th century, stock prices have slumped at the beginning of every major war and with serious threats of imminent conflict. Once the wars started and the dimensions of hostilities and the demands of defense became known, the markets rallied but did not turn in stellar performances. When the wars ended, the markets slumped before anticipating the return to a peacetime economy. There are so many social, political and economic forces in a wartime situation that the effects of news may be conflicting or may cancel each other out. Neither the hawkish nor the dovish view of Wall Street and war has proved to be a way to profit in the markets.

While broad social movements are not likely to be changed by specific or episodic news, it is possible to categorize good and bad business news. Markets perceive and react to the following good corporate news:

- An increase in revenue
- An increase in earnings
- Raised or initiated dividends
- Stock splits
- Takeover bids or the acquisition of a company above the market price
- An increase of cash or capital assets
- A decrease of debt
- The discovery of a natural resource
- Price increases
- The introduction of a new product
- An increase in research and development
- Government agency approval of a product or pricing
- Foreign licensing
- New senior management
- A positive media story on a company

And markets perceive and react to bad corporate news such as:

- A decrease in revenue
- A decrease in earnings
- Lowered or omitted dividends
- A reverse stock split
- Acquiring another company at a premium
- A decrease in cash or capital assets
- An increase of debt
- Price decreases
- Labor strife
- A reduced market share
- A decrease in research and development
- Government agency denial or disapproval of a product or pricing

- Patent infringement or litigation
- The death of a highly regarded chief executive officer
- A negative media story on a company

The Sell Side

Understanding the implications of business news is an important factor in forecasting the prices of securities. There is a natural, though unspoken, bias in reporting on business, especially on corporate news. Most of what goes into print or is heard and seen in the electronic media is powerfully positive. Companies do not hire high-powered public relations firms to wash their dirty laundry in public.

In recent years, the value of imagery has become so apparent and the sensitivity of companies so heightened that it has become increasingly rare for negative stories to appear. Local newspapers have killed stories that are critical of major advertisers, and important national dailies and magazines have run any number of puff pieces. A poor performance by a company or industry is handled tardily, if at all, and the difficulties are usually blamed on factors unrelated to management—from labor and union problems to unrestricted imports. Only when the company or industry is mired in such deep trouble that it can no longer be ignored does that condition make news.

With that in mind, it is hard to get a balanced, realistic picture. There are always dozens of reasons to buy shares, but precious few reasons to sell them, at least in the public media.

This lopsidedness is a major concern for investors and speculators, for it is reinforced by the brokerage industry and investment banking.

Brokerage house recommendations account for volumes of trading activity. But just how valuable are they in gaining on the market? Are they worth more than the paper they are printed on? Efficient market theorists would say no—everything known is already in the price. However, a recent study by Kent Womack, a financial economist at Dartmouth, indicates otherwise. In a working paper, "Do Brokerage Analysts' Recommendations Have Investment Value?" he pointed out that in an analysis of 1,500 buy-sell recommendations from 14 top stockbrokers over a three-year period, the price of a stock rose 3 percent (over any market change), while sell recommendations saw a fall of 4.7 percent. Nor did prices drift back to original levels, as previously thought. But recommendations moved up an additional 2.4 percent the next month, with the gains still apparent a year later.

On the sell side, the recommendations were down 13.8 percent after six months. Good analysts clearly have a keen sense of mispriced securities. Perhaps the more significant moves on the downside have to do with the simple fact that in relative terms there are so few of them. Brokers rarely say "sell." More often they mark a security to "hold" or give it a neutral rating. No doubt they are cautious about their future investment banking relations and/or the ability of the analyst to revisit the company in question after a negative rating.

Nevertheless, the history of financial markets suggests that in absolute terms, they go down almost as often as they go up. And, in relative terms, in an inflationary period they go down more often. An investor with holdings in the Dow Jones Industrial Average (DJIA) in 1966, when the market touched 1,000 for the first time, would have had a number of other chances in the 1960s, 70s and 80s to get out more or less even. However, the DJIA did not make a significant breakthrough until the 1982–83 bull market. In relative terms— that is, accounting for inflation—the DJIA would have had to exceed 2,400 to retain its purchasing power.

There are times to invest, and there are times to be out of the market, or on the short side. Professional money managers do not always employ strict formulas to tell them when to get out of the market; often they react like everyone else and watch profitable positions melt away. Market homilies offer some folk wisdom, such as "buy on the rumor and sell on the news" or "the first loss is the cheapest loss," but few credible guidelines. The most common one may be categorized as the "down 15 percent (or 10 percent or 20 percent) and out" strategy. In other words if the price declines 15 percent below the purchase price or subsequent highs, a stock is immediately sold. This approach, if followed too rigidly, may lead to being whipsawed, being sold out, in a volatile market.

Another tactic, somewhat less rigid, is to establish a time frame and a target price. This approach assumes that in the future the stock will reach a fair price, one considerably higher than the purchase, or "undervalued," price. When the target is reached, the sell trigger is pulled. While the procedure leaves an investor less open to whipsawing, its mechanical nature may prompt him to sell out a position that is in the midst of a strong advance. Others relying on the appropriate rate of return concept expect to net a 10 percent, 15 percent or 20 percent annual increment before selling.

Some money managers sell call options on the shares as they reach their targets. Should the advance peter out, they still have the shares, plus a premium. On the other hand, if the price continues to rise, the shares will be called away, leaving the seller with both principal and premium. Still other techniques call for selling part of a position as it increases in price, say half when the price doubles, and leaving the remainder as a cost-free bonus, so to speak, without immediate tax liability. And a number of money managers and individuals prefer to keep their eye on the balance of their respective portfolios; if the equity position increases above a stipulated level, they either sell a percentage or invest new monies in the fixed-interest side.

Whichever sell discipline is used, selling is intimately tied to news, especially bad news. There is no magical bad-news formula for selling stock, but some sophisticated investors claim they "never believe a rumor until it is officially denied." Perhaps that's not a bad start. Others are willing to live with one piece of poor corporate news, but use the appearance of a second item as confirmation of a weakening psychological environment. Since news makes the market go, to paraphrase an old saying, you can't be too rich or too knowledgeable!

GLOSSARY

acid-test ratio In a time of trouble, how much cash could a corporation generate by converting its current assets? Would it be enough to cover its current liabilities? The acid-test ratio is arrived at by adding cash and marketable securities. This measure of corporate liquidity is also known as "quick assets."

accrued interest The amount of interest due on a bond or other obligation since it was last paid. A buyer of a bond will pay the purchase price plus whatever interest is due since the last payment. However, some bonds are traded "flat," with no adjustment for accrued interest, since the issuer of the bond is either in default or in some other difficulty.

ADR (American depositary receipt) A substitute certificate for foreign shares. Issued by American banks against the bearer securities of a foreign corporation that are held on deposit, the ADR is as freely negotiable as a domestic certificate. Such receipts are issued only on widely held and traded corporations. The issuing banks provide the holders of ADRs with all pertinent corporate information, such as annual reports, stock dividends and subscription rights. They also provide the holder with dollars instead of foreign currency for dividend disbursements and sale of rights. Hundreds of foreign corporations have ADRs issued against their securities. Most ADRs are traded in the over-the-counter market.

amortization The payment of a debt over a fixed period, usually on an installment basis. These prorated payments on a mortgage over 10, 20 or 30 years include the repayment of both principal and interest. In the early years of the mortgage, most of the repayment is interest; in the final years most of the repayment is principal. On a corporate bond issue, amortization is provided for through some form of sinking fund. Periodic payments are made to the fund so that the debt can be retired early or at its redemption date.

arbitrage The simultaneous buying and selling of currencies, commodities or securities in different markets with the hope of profiting from price differentials. In free markets, price discrepancies continually arise, and professional traders in banks and brokerage houses attempt to take advantage of these rate fluctuations. These actions ensure a relative parity of prices wherever these items are actively traded. In takeovers or acquisitions, arbitrage traders will buy the presumed target, the company to be acquired, in order to exchange the shares for risk-free appreciation from the acquiring company.

asking price The price at which a seller is willing to part with his securities. An asking or offering price in the over-the-counter market is the latter price when the security is quoted. Thus "10–11" simply means that the market maker is asking or offering shares at $11, but is willing to bid or pay only $10 for new nventory.

assets Everything a company owns or is owed. Usually assets are divided into current assets, fixed assets and intangible fixed assets. Current assets consist of cash, accounts receivable and inventory. Fixed assets are brick and mortar, equipment, land and natural resources. Intangible fixed assets are good will, patents, trademarks, copyrights and franchises. Working capital is usually the excess of current assets over current liabilities.

at the market A customer's authorization to his broker to obtain the best prevailing price for his order at the time the order is given.

auction market The stock exchanges hold auction markets in securities when there is ample liquidity, or a plentiful supply of buyers and sellers. In such circumstances, the specialist performs only the function of matching orders. But a specialist is also charged with "making a market"; that is, he buys and sells for his own account when there aren't enough buyers or sellers. The auction market is in contrast to the over-the-counter market, where prices are negotiated between buyers and sellers and each is dealing for his own account.

balance of payments A statement of a nation's international transactions. It is not so much a balance sheet as a profit and loss statement. It does not deal in totals, but in flow of funds. The balance of payments measures the transfer of resources and assets both in and out of a country. At best, the figures are approximate, since there are many pitfalls and unknown transactions. Nevertheless, despite its imperfections, the balance of payments is a critical measure of a nation's international standing, the health of its economy and the value of its currency. A surplus or deficit in the balance of payments can be measured in several ways, but there are two primary ones. The first is the "official reserve transaction basis"—the increase or decrease of the U.S. official reserve assets of gold, convertible currencies, the International Monetary Fund gold tranche and obligations held by official foreign bodies such as central banks. The second way is on a "liquidity basis"—the increase or decrease of official reserve assets in addition to short-term (less than one year) liquid obligations held abroad, both private and official. Running huge deficits or huge surpluses causes instability in international money markets, for they are a reflection of overvaluation or undervaluation of currencies.

balance sheet First used extensively in Venice during the Renaissance, the modern balance sheet is a statement of a business's assets, liabilities and equity capital for specific dates. Presented in tabular form, the basic balance sheet formula is assets equal liabilities plus equity capital. To put it another way, to determine the shareholder equity, subtract liabilities from assets to find the equity capital.

bankruptcy The state of insolvency in which a person or corporation is unable to meet the just claims of creditors. Corporate debtors can seek the protection of the courts by petitioning for voluntary bankruptcy, or creditors can petition for a condition of involuntary bankruptcy for the debtor. The court takes over the assets either to satisfy the creditors to some degree by selling the remaining assets or to protect the business while it undergoes reorganization.

bear A bear is anyone who believes stock prices are due to decline. He makes money by selling short—selling his own or borrowed stock with the hope of replacing it at a lower level. However, when there is a general feeling of bearishness in the marketplace, investors tend not to sell short, but rather to leave the marketplace or refrain from committing any new money to investments.

bearer bond   *See* **registered bond.**

beta coefficient   This is a measure of volatility, reached by comparing the price action of individual stocks with the market as a whole. A beta coefficient of 1 means that the stock and the general market move together, that they have identical percentage increases. A coefficient of 2 indicates that the stock fluctuates twice as much as the market.

bid price   *See* **asking price.**

Big Board   A term for the New York Stock Exchange, the country's leading exchange, where 2,904 different companies are traded. Once a company meets the exchange's requirements, it has joined the corporate big league. However, some giants of industry that could easily meet these requirements are not traded on the Big Board. They prefer the over-the-counter market either due to the nature of that market or because they prefer to remain a privately held family corporation.

blue chip   An expression for a high-quality security. A blue chip company has a long and respectable fiscal history, constant dividends, stable earning power and a sound future.

blue-sky law   State regulatory laws concerning the sale of securities, as distinct from the federal statutes. Practically all states have laws aimed at, in the words of an early judgment, "speculative schemes which have no more basis than so many feet of the blue sky."

bond   An IOU from a corporation or government agency that promises to pay back to the lender the full amount, or par value, of the loan at a given maturity date plus a fixed rate of interest on a periodic schedule. Since bonds are essentially promissory notes to lenders, they do not represent ownership. The lenders, holders of the bonds, are creditors of the business. The issuance of bonds creates a trust indenture, or deed of trust, which establishes a trustee to represent the bondholders. The indenture contains a series of provisions outlining the conditions of the bond issue. Banks usually serve as trustees.

book value The true value of all corporate assets, less liabilities, gives a historic view of what it cost to establish the business. This is a particularly important consideration in times of inflation, when it costs far more to replace assets. In short, the book value is a sum of the past rather than an assessment of the present. Perhaps a closer estimate of a business's worth is the market value, the value placed on the company equity in the securities markets. Investors are less interested in book value—one doesn't make an investment on the basis of a liquidator's appraisal—than in profit potential. For that reason, current market value is deemed a better guide.

bucket shops and boiler rooms Shady brokerage houses and high-pressure dealers in mythical or highly speculative securities.

bull An optimist who foresees better business conditions and rising stock prices.

call *See* **option.**

callable bonds Many bond issues have a callable feature. They can be retired or redeemed at the option of the corporation. Sometime in the future it may benefit the issuer to eliminate a portion of his outstanding debt by restructuring the capitalization or simply to effect a savings on interest by refunding. From the investor's point of view, a callable provision is anathema unless there are certain safeguards. Having purchased high-yielding, long-term bonds, he does not wish to switch horses in midstream, for almost assuredly he will not be able to replace them at comparable yields. He can protect himself by purchasing only bonds with call protection, a provision that the issue will not be called for 5, 10 or 20 years. Further protection exists in issues that pay a premium over par should the issue be called.

capital The term originally derived from the Latin word *caput*, for "head," and probably referred to the earliest Greek coins. These coins, circa 555 B.C., had heads of Greek deities on one side and the owl and the olive branch on the other. Capital in the private sector is money used to invest: to initiate a company, to expand plant and equipment or to acquire other assets. Owners of capital customarily use their funds to provide for a return on capital employed. If a company cannot project a reasonable return on the capital it seeks, it is doubtful that it should undertake the venture for which the new capital is to be used.

capital gains   The profit realized on the sale of securities or other assets. For tax purposes, a long-term capital gain (with favorable tax treatment) is one held more than one year.

cash flow   The net income from earnings plus expenses that do not use cash, such as depreciation, amortization and depletion. This flow of funds through the corporation is a measure of its ability to meet its expenses, dividends and potential new funding.

certificate of deposit   A bank issues a certificate of deposit for receipt of a sum on a time deposit, usually between three months and three years. These certificates, called CDs, earn interest at maturity, are negotiable and, if they are in the six-figure range, are easily traded in a secondary market. CDs were first issued in 1961 to attract short-term corporate funds that otherwise would have been invested in government bills, commercial paper or other short-term securities. Since 1983, banks have been free to offer a wide range of CDs, paying money market rates for as little as $500.

churning   When the market lacks a dominant trend but buying and selling is extremely active, the market is churning. If your broker is a churner, it will cost you money, for he makes a commission on each purchase and sale while your position remains substantially unchanged.

closed-end investment company   A mutual fund that, unlike the majority, raises a fixed amount of capital to invest. Once the capital is raised, the fund does not stand ready to sell further shares or redeem those already sold. Its shares are frequently listed and traded on the exchanges. Market quotations of closed-end funds may vary greatly from the underlying net as set value of their shares. On occasion, shares can be purchased at great discounts from their actual worth. This is particularly true in depressed markets.

The City   London's financial district, occasionally known as "the square mile" and a center of world finance. It is a prime market for Eurodollars, international insurance, gold, metals and international lending.

collateral   An asset that is pledged as security for a loan.

commodity transactions Dealings on organized exchanges in contracts on crops, provisions or products. The contracts are standard: They are fixed with regard to the item, the quality and the quantity. The only variables are the month of delivery and the price. While there are spot markets for commodities—buying and selling for immediate cash—the commodity exchanges deal in futures contracts. The purpose of a contract is to protect producer and consumer from untoward price fluctuations. By means of a futures contract they can establish their costs. Because prices do fluctuate and conditions are uncertain, commodity contracts are actively traded with substantial price differentials. It is this volatility that attracts hedgers and speculators.

common stock Common stock, or shares, represents fractional ownership of a business enterprise. The first companies to be formed on the basis of mutual ownership were founded in Holland in the 17th century to foster foreign trade. The earliest stock company was the Associate East India Company. Its shares were registered subscriptions of varying amounts and were no sooner issued than the commercially minded Dutch started to trade them. Today, unless their shares are specifically classified as nonvoting stock (usually termed Class B common), common stock holders are able to vote in the election of a board of directors and on other corporate matters at stockholder meetings. Common stock holders have the right to dividends when declared by the board, the right to subscribe to new issues of stock before outsiders, the right to protect the corporation against improper management through derivative actions, the right to transfer their holdings freely and the right to share in the proceeds in case of dissolution of the business.

compound interest A discovery of the Italian Renaissance that is aptly expressed by the saying, "Money makes money and the money money makes makes more money." In other words, the interest earned during a fixed period is converted or added to the principal. The new principal is then the base figure for calculating interest for the subsequent period. A formula that describes compound interest calculations is: $F = P(1 + R) T$, in which F is the total future repayment value of a loan (principal plus the total accumulated or compound interest); P is the principal; R is the rate of interest per year, or annual percentage rate; and T is time in years.

convertible bonds Owners of convertible bonds have the privilege of exchanging them for a fixed number of shares. Investors will convert bonds to stocks when the stock market is having a boom. During a recession, they feel safer with their funds in "converts" since the yield tends to act as a floor on the price of the instrument.

corner Through massive buying of a security or a commodity, usually by a pool of speculators, buyers achieve a monopoly. They can then dictate the price and terms of delivery. Today, securities laws and the SEC make it virtually impossible to achieve a corner, though the Hunt interests came close in 1980 with silver.

debenture A bond without collateral or property behind it. A company issues this promissory note on nothing more than its reputation and general credit, pledging to pay interest and redeem it at maturity. As with garden-variety bonds, debentures are issued under a trust indenture with specific terms.

depletion The gradual exhaustion of a natural resource that is fundamental to a business's operation, such as a mine, an oil well or a mineral deposit. Depletion is considered a return of capital from the earnings of a wasting asset. As such, a depletion allowance is a deductible business expense for tax purposes. The government encourages exploration through substantial depletion allowances.

depreciation Wear and tear on capital assets. Since everything eventually runs down, except land, the managers of a business must allocate the cost of plant and machinery during their useful life. One common way to allocate such costs is on a straight line, with equal payments. If a numerical machine tool has a useful life of five years, it is reasonable to deduct 20 percent of its original value each year. Should a company deduct all the cost in the year of purchase, it would depress earnings, perhaps dramatically, in that year. In times of inflation, depreciation tends to be underestimated, since it will cost more to replace equipment than it did to buy it. Depreciation is usually calculated in constant dollars, not in current ones, though some enlightened companies now use both methods. Thus inadequate monies are set aside for replacement. During a period of inflation companies run down their capital assets, since they are allocating insufficient funds for new capital equipment. However, by insufficient depreciation corporations have paid too much in taxes, since by the same token they have overstated their earnings.

derivatives   Securities that derive their value from underlying securities. A package of derivatives, in combination, is used by institutions to hedge against exposures to interest rate fluctuations, currency fluctuations or other financial liability.

dilution   Watering stock may take several forms, from the outright and illegal running of a printing press to subtle and sophisticated acquisition techniques. Any recapitalization of a corporation that reduces the proportionate interest of the stockholder without due compensation is a form of dilution. A rights offering will usually extend to all the equity owners a chance to maintain their interest should they wish to participate in the new financing. If they do not, then they may sell the rights.

disclosure   The organic laws of the present securities business are a series of acts passed by Congress in the 1930s and 1940s. While the acts, particularly the Securities Act of 1933 and the Securities Exchange Act of 1934, are specific as to what may be done and how, their underlying effectiveness rests on full disclosure of relevant information. If the investor has all the facts available about a given situation, he can act intelligently and appropriately—or at least in his own self-interest. While the theory is simple, in practice it is less so, since honorable men and women can and do disagree as to what is material and what is not. Nevertheless, the SEC does require annual or periodic reports on more than 6,000 publicly owned companies. Those reports are available to the public from either the SEC, the company in question or one of the private reporting services. Some of the more important reports are: 10K, annual reports; 10-Q, quarterly income statements; 8-K, unscheduled material events; 13-D, a 5 percent investment position; proxy statements; insider trading.

discount rate   A major tool of the Federal Reserve System for controlling credit. To tighten credit, the Fed raises the discount rate—the rate at which member banks can borrow from a Fed bank to increase their reserves. The bank places with the Fed bank some form of eligible paper as collateral. The government will keep raising the discount rate in an effort to slow down an economy that is expanding too quickly on the theory that businesses will borrow less as rates go up. To stimulate business the Fed will drop the discount rate, allowing banks to borrow cheaply and increase their reserves.

dividends   A portion of the profits, paid by the corporation, after taxes, to the stockholders. The owners of equity are not necessarily entitled to dividends; the decision is up to the board of directors. Should the corporation pay a dividend, the recipient must also pay income taxes on that money. While it is possible to receive tax-free dividends if they are really a return on capital, dividends from most stock issues are taxable. In the past, since stocks were considered riskier, corporations kept the dividend yields high to make them attractive. Conversely, since bonds were secure, their coupon yields could be kept low. This historic differential disappeared in the 1960s, and bonds presently pay higher yields than equity.

Dow Theory   A theory of stock market movements originally enunciated by Charles Dow, a founder of the *Wall Street Journal,* and codified by William P. Hamilton and Robert Rhea. Presently a short-term guide to stock prices, but originally conceived as a technique of forecasting the business cycle. The Dow Jones Industrial Average (composed of 30 manufacturing companies) is an index of the nation's productive potential, and the Transportation Average (composed of 20 companies) is an indication of the volume of goods being transported. They must reinforce each other to validate the direction of the business cycle. They confirm each other by both making new highs or new lows. If they take separate paths, or if the preceding lows are violated after making new highs, a reversal is in the works. The trend has been broken.

due diligence study   Before a public underwriting of a company's securities, the investment banking house conducting the sale must examine the business thoroughly. It must research all the elements that go into the registration prospectus: product, competition, marketability, risk, ownership, financing, etc. The due diligence study is an integral part of preparing material to comply with full disclosure requirements.

earnings per share   A key measurement of a corporation's profitability vis-à-vis its share price. Earnings per share is calculated by taking the company's net income for the year, after taxes and dividends on the preferred stock, and dividing by the number of common shares outstanding. Thus, if the net income was half a million dollars and the company had issued one million shares, the earnings per share would be 50 cents. Not only do earnings change, but the number of shares outstanding may vary from year to year. Furthermore, it is important to appreciate what the earnings per share would be if all convertible instruments, options and warrants were converted. Many corporations publish two sets of figures: earnings on a current basis and earnings on a fully diluted one.

easy-money policy Monetary objectives of the Federal Reserve System tend to be either expansionary or constrictive with regard to the money supply. Depending on the targets set by the Federal Open Market Committee, the Reserve System attempts to manipulate the supply accordingly. For instance, if the committee is concerned about the slow expansion of M1 (currency plus demand deposits of the public), it will press for the outright purchase of government obligations from the banking system. This action will supply the banks with abundant reserves, thus forcing down interest rates, especially in the short-term market. This easy-money policy sets the tone for the economy, but its stimulating effect can be inflationary if pursued too long.

equipment trust certificates A form of promissory note issued against the purchase of specific transportation equipment—usually railroad locomotives. A trustee purchases the equipment for certificate shares and rents it to the railroad. The certificates are then sold by the manufacturer or seller of the equipment to the investing public. Some equipment trust certificates are listed on the exchanges and are regarded as reasonably secure fixed-interest obligations, though not of prime quality.

equity *See* **common stock.**

Eurodollars/Eurocurrencies Eurocurrencies are generally taken to mean currencies on deposit in foreign banks—that is, in banks to which the currencies are not native. The typical and most prominent example is the American greenback. Dollars held by Germans in German banks are considered Eurodollars. Eurocurrencies do not have to be European currencies or owned by Europeans. The term stands for domestic convertible currencies deposited abroad, be they Japanese yen, Swiss francs or pounds sterling. Dollars make up approximately 80 percent of the Eurocurrency market. Since the currencies are freely convertible, they are in essence outside the monetary restrictions that govern their domestic equivalents; these currencies constitute but a single pool. Eurocurrencies are used in two distinct fashions. On a short-term basis, they are lent through a network of bank credits. Minimum loans, whose rates are determined by the London Interbank Offered Rate (LIBOR), are usually half a million dollars. On a long-term basis, Eurocurrencies have made it possible to develop a Eurobond market with the sale of bonds denominated in one or a basket of currencies. Numerous American corporations have taken advantage of this source of funds for their international requirements.

exchange controls   Exchange controls have numerous guises, but their function is to restrict the free exchange or convertibility of a nation's currency. For instance, a country with a shortage of hard currency or gold for international transactions will rule that all receipts from its export trade must be turned over to the central bank. It then limits the sale of foreign currencies, effectively cutting off imports or limiting them to items approved by the government. Such a situation enables a government to equalize its balance of payments or even build a surplus in its reserves. But at the same time, it has assumed a form of exchange controls that has made its currency not only less desirable but probably inconvertible. Foreign traders are not likely to accept such currency if they cannot turn around and repurchase other currencies. This in turn causes a black market price for the currency, one that reflects the true supply-and-demand situation of the currency rather than one determined by the government. Indeed, one of the objectives of exchange controls is to regulate the parity values of a nation's currency. However, such a step puts the currency under a cloud and invariably disturbs trade transactions.

ex-dividend   A dividend is declared for stockholders of record as of a certain date, though it may be payable several weeks later. Anyone owning the security as of the record date, not the date of distribution, receives the dividend, even if he sells it between the record date and the distribution date. The price of the shares will usually reflect the passing of the record date when stockholders then sell ex-dividends by some adjustment downward to compensate the buyer for missing the dividend.

face value   The amount written on the front of a financial instrument and ostensibly its true value. However, a $1,000 bond is not necessarily worth $1,000; it could be selling at a premium or at a discount, depending on maturity dates and interest rates. About the only time a bond's market value definitely equals its face value is on its maturity date.

federal funds   Sight claims or demand deposits of member banks of the Federal Reserve System on deposit with a Federal Reserve bank. Commercial banks lend these funds to each other when they find their reserve position has run down. It is usually cheaper to borrow these funds than to apply to the Fed's discount window. Such funds are lent on a daily basis and are a bellwether for the direction of interest rates.

fill or kill   A limit order that must be executed immediately, completely and at the price called for when it is received or canceled.

fixed assets   Everything needed by a corporation to produce and sell its goods and services. All the property, plant, equipment, furniture, trucks, etc. (with a life span exceeding one year) are usually regarded as fixed assets. The cost of these assets less the depreciation accumulated to date is their balance sheet valuation.

flat   Bonds whose issuers are for some reason unable to pay the authorized interest are traded flat. This is also true of some bonds whose interest payments depend on company earnings. In general, no allowance is made for interest payments since none exist, unlike the usual procedure of compensating the seller for whatever interest was earned since the last payment period.

forward contract   Forward contracts are not traded on exchanges like future contracts since they are not standardized as to units covered, quality of product or day of delivery. Forward contracts are usually customized for individual clients. Thus, in foreign exchange transactions, a buyer of a forward contract from a bank can specify the exact amount of the currency needed and precisely when it is needed. On a commodity exchange, the purchaser of a foreign currency futures contract could receive only an approximation of his needs if he did take delivery.

fundamentals   Financial analysts are divided between the fundamentalists and the technicians. The fundamentalists, who are in the majority, firmly believe that a knowledge of the basic company and industry affords the only reliable information upon which to act. It follows that buying and selling securities depends on understanding the business and the financial yardsticks. Technicians, on the other hand, believe that the proper way to study securities is to follow the stock prices. They don't negate the fundamentals, but they find the "footprints in the sand" more revealing.

funded debt   Long-term debt represented by bonds compared with current debt or liabilities that are not backed by such obligations. The greater the percentage of funded debt in the capital structure of a corporation, the more leverage available to the equity. However, it is not a good practice to have more debt than working capital (current assets less current liabilities). If funded debt grows to more than 50 percent of a company's capitalization, there may be problems in servicing the debt.

futures   A futures contract in commodity trading calls for the specific amount and grade of commodity to be delivered some time in the future. Most futures contracts expire in 1 to 17 months. Commodity contracts are hedges against uncertainty, a way of fixing costs ahead of time. Most of them are never fulfilled, but are closed out by offsetting transactions.

general obligation bonds   Municipalities can issue bonds backed by their power to levy and collect taxes from their residents. Such bonds put the municipalities' full faith and credit on the line, and are usually considered preeminent tax-free securities

going public   Shorthand for a public underwriting by an investment banking firm of a hitherto private corporation. While the company could sell its own shares directly to the public, and some do, the more conventional way is to hire an investment banker. He will either buy the whole issue himself, and then undertake to sell it, or form a syndicate with other investment bankers to sell the shares jointly, buying whatever part of the issue is not purchased to stabilize its price. If the issue is highly speculative, new, and/or without a track record, the underwriter will not buy the shares outright, but will sell them for the company on a "best efforts" basis.

gold fixing   Twice a day, five bullion dealers in London set an equilibrium price for gold that is a guideline for international trading.

good till canceled   A market order to a broker marked "g.t.c." will remain as an open order on the books of the specialist until it is either filled at the required price or killed by request of the principal.

indenture A legal contract that a borrowing corporation enters into with a trustee (usually a bank), who represents the bond-holders. The trust indenture backs up the promises of the bond certificate and is the basis of legal action should the corporation default on its bonds.

inflation A rapid rise in prices and wages or, conversely, a rapid fall in the value of money. In general, there are two types of inflation, a cost-push and a demand-pull. The former occurs when costs advance quickly due to shortages in raw materials and other supplies. The latter occurs when public demand forces prices higher and the inventory is unable to expand quickly enough to keep prices stable. Three elements keep inflation active: Demand must exceed supply so that higher prices do not result in lost sales; the public must assume that future prices will be higher than current ones so that there is good and sufficient reason to buy now rather than later; and finally, there must be an abundant and perpetually increasing money supply to pay for all the goods and services. Any one of these factors is inflationary, but taken together, they virtually guarantee an upward spiral.

initial margin In commodities trading, a trader is required to put up a good-faith deposit or initial margin before establishing a position. Should the original deposit become inadequate due to adverse price moves, he will be required to supplement that first deposit with a maintenance margin.

institutional investor While individuals still own the majority of corporate shares, institutions do the bulk of the trading on the exchanges. Hundreds of financial (and other) institutions are responsible for over two-thirds of share transactions.

interest Interest is rent paid for the use of someone else's money. The amount of interest is determined by the interest rate, usually expressed as a percentage per year. The level of interest rates often helps determine the direction of the stock market. When rates are very high, fixed-interest securities become very competitive and some funds leave the stock market for the high yields obtainable in the bond market. Conversely, low interest rates tend to make money plentiful, a prime condition for a rising stock market.

investment banker Investment bankers raise equity capital for companies undertaking initial public offerings of their stock. Depending on the size of the issue, they provide the risk capital themselves or in conjunction with other investment bankers, who form a syndicate. They are also instrumental in underwriting federal agency and corporate bond issues. In addition, investment bankers provide financial expertise for corporations in matters of mergers, acquisitions and reorganizations.

investment companies   *See* **open-end investment company.**

leverage   For an ancient Greek it was a fulcrum and a stick, which if it was long enough could move the world. For the modern investor it is the advantage, or disadvantage, of a company using an inordinate amount of debt to effect equity disproportionately. The inherent multiplier of leverage magnifies changes in earnings. Leverage is also attendant with margin buying. If one can borrow 50 percent, the rate of return is leveraged, or magnified, by a factor of two.

limit order   A limit order, whether to buy or to sell, restricts the broker from executing a customer's order at a disadvantage— that is, above what he wished to pay or less than he wished to sell.

liquidity   A central factor for decent markets in a free-enterprise system. With liquidity, one can buy and sell assets or services at a moment's notice. Moreover, price changes from transaction to transaction will be minimal, reflecting only new information and the imbalance of supply and demand.

load fee   Some mutual funds, or open-end investment companies, charge a sales fee with which to pay distributors and brokers for their efforts in selling the funds. These sales charges, or load fees, can range from 1 percent to 8.5 percent. A number of mutual funds sell no load funds; there is no selling charge, but the consumer must contact the fund directly to purchase its shares. There is no evidence that funds with load fees perform any better than those without them.

long   To buy stock is to go long. Its opposite is to sell stocks you own or borrow, to go short.

long-term   Assets held for more than one year are considered long-term holdings for the purpose of taxes. Under the present law, tax rates are more favorable for long-term capital gains than for short-term gains.

Ms (M1, M2, M3)   Defining money is a tricky business at best, but central bankers and economists have an even more difficult job in tracking the money supply. It is generally appreciated by all schools of economists, investors and public officials that it is of critical importance, since too little growth leads to stagnation and too much growth leads to inflation. But the exact nature of the money supply is illusory since it varies from transaction money to savings, the former being exceedingly important while the latter is far less so, since it isn't being used. To categorize the different kinds—a harder job now that financial deregulation has made it easy to move from savings to transactions and back again—the Federal Reserve uses three Ms. M1 measures only cash, checking accounts and all forms of demand deposits even if they earn interest; M2 includes M1 plus money market funds and somewhat less liquid holdings; M3 is both M1 and M2 and financial instruments less easily converted into cash. Finally, this is topped off with "L," a broad measurement that encompasses securities maturing within 18 months. When the money supply as measured by M1 is on target (in line with Fed projections), there is peace in the money markets.

maintenance margin   *See* **initial margin.**

margin call   If you borrow brokers' funds to buy or sell securities, a margin call may eventually catch up to you if prices move adversely. In recent years, 50 percent margin rates have enabled investors and speculators to borrow $1 for every $1 of their own. They could buy (or sell) $10,000 of securities for $5,000. If the value fell to $6,600, they would receive a margin call (via telephone or telegram), for the broker's maintenance margin of 25 percent was threatened. At $6,600, a sale of the securities would enable the broker to recapture his $5,000, but the remaining value, $1,600, has already begun to violate the maintenance margin.

market makers   While sometimes used to indicate a specialist on an exchange, more frequently the term refers to a dealer in the over-the-counter market who stands ready to trade a number of issues. Remember, he is buying wholesale and selling retail, and always for his own account. Thus it is possible to haggle or negotiate over the price.

market order   An order to a broker to buy at the market—that is, to buy at the offered or asked price or sell at whatever the bid price is at the moment the order is received.

maturity The date upon which a debt obligation becomes due. The original maturity is the total number of years in which the obligation will be redeemed by the issuer, while current maturity refers to the number of years from the present to its redemption. Short maturities are usually less than a year; medium maturities are from 1 to 10 years; and long maturities are from 10 to 30 years.

money market funds Mutual funds that have in their portfolios, not stocks, but money market instruments: certificates of deposit, commercial paper, U.S. Treasury and federal agencies' bills and notes, and bankers' acceptances. While the mix varies from fund to fund, the components of these funds are the low-risk, highly liquid debt of major banks, businesses and the federal government, with relatively short maturity dates. While the underlying components are sold in the open market, their minimum size is usually on the order of six figures. Money market funds buy them, but then sell shares in these funds for a dollar a unit. Thus the small investor can obtain almost the same yield, after a fractional management charge, as a large one.

money market rates In a free marketplace, the rates at which money can be borrowed or lent, whether overnight or for longer maturities. Before financial deregulation, only large investors could obtain money market rates; today, even the smallest investor can obtain rates comparable to institutional funds.

municipals A general reference to tax-free bonds issued by municipalities, state and regional agencies, local units of government and even school districts and water works. Municipals fall into two broad categories: general obligation bonds, which are backed by the full faith and credit of the issuer, and revenue bonds, which obtain their stream of income from the fees (revenues) collected by the project or authority that issued them. Since these bonds have tax-free yields, their coupon rates are below market rates for taxable bonds. For the investor, the final consideration is not the coupon rate but the after-tax yield.

negotiable instrument No one is quite sure whether it was the medieval Arabs or Jews who invented the first substitute for cash, but whoever it was gave the world a valuable addition to money. A negotiable instrument—a check, draft, promissory note, bill of exchange, certificate of deposit—is like money but can have some special advantages as well. In general, there are four basic conditions for a negotiable instrument: It must be payable on demand to the order of the bearer or someone else; it must be in writing and authenticated by the drawer or maker; it must be an unconditional promise to pay a fixed sum of money; and it must be payable on demand or at a fixed future time.

negotiated market   *See* **auction market.**

net worth   An individual's assets less his liabilities and debts. The net worth of a company is a summary of its capitalization—the original value of its shares when issued, any present value above that previously declared value or capital surplus, and finally any earned surplus, or earnings retained by the company after dividend payments. Net worth is also referred to as the stockholders' equity; when divided by the number of shares outstanding, the result is the book value per share.

odd lot   *See* **round lot.**

open-end investment company   A mutual fund that may issue any number of shares on the basis of its net asset value. A closed-end investment company has a fixed number of shares. Some closed-end companies are listed on the exchanges and can occasionally sell at a significant discount from their underlying assets

open interest   Every time a futures contract is entered into, the open interest in that commodity is increased by one. Conversely, every time a futures contract is closed out, the open interest is decreased by one. The open interest in a given contract is simply a reflection of volume activity in that commodity that month.

open order   An order given to a broker that calls for execution at a certain price or better. Such an order remains open on the broker's books until it is executed or canceled. Thus, it is sometimes referred to as "good till canceled."

options   Contracts that give the purchaser the right (but not the obligation) to buy or sell a set number of shares (usually 100) at a set price within a given period of time. Naturally, an option that conveys such a right has a price; the price for which it sells reflects the amount of time left to exercise the option and the striking or contract price at which the right can be exercised. Besides listed options of shares, options have sprung up on a wide range of financial futures, indexes and commodities.

Options command great leverage, since for a small purchase price the contract gives temporary control of the underlying product and its profit potential.

par value   The original issue value of a company's shares. Within a short operating history that figure becomes fiction, in no way related to the actual value due to earnings, acquisitions, and recapitalizations. Consequently, companies set the par value at either no-par value or at a figure so low as to suggest that it is essentially meaningless. In the bond market, par value is the face value of the bond, to be paid at maturity.

pass-through securities   Pools of government mortgages, especially the Government National Mortgage Association (GNMA) and the Federal Home Loan Mortgage Corporation (FHMC), are the underlying securities for pass-through certificates. Purchasers of such registered issues receive payment of interest and principal, issued monthly, for the life of the underlying mortgages, usually about 12 years.

pay-out ratio   Companies establish policies on what percentage of net earnings will be held for corporate purposes and what percentage paid out to stockholders in dividends. For many years the ratio was 50/50, but in recent years some very rapidly growing companies have plowed back all their earnings into expansion.

pink sheets   Daily compilations by the National Quotation Bureau of market prices for most of the over-the-counter shares that are not reported by the National Association of Securities Dealers Automated Quotation System (Nasdaq) or other listings in the press. The sheets give not only the price but the spreads of all the dealers making a market in a given issue.

preferred stock   Preferred stock receives dividends before common stock in the sense that it has prior claim and so must be serviced before the common can be considered. If the preferred issue has the additional privilege of being cumulative, it also receives dividends that may have been passed over the previous year due to poor earnings. Again, it receives back dividends, as well as current ones, before the common.

prime rate   The interest rate charged by commercial banks to their most creditworthy business customers. This is another bellwether for investors, revealing a tightening or loosening of the money supply.

private offering   A public company (even a private one) can make a private offering to 35 or fewer sophisticated, affluent investors in order to raise money. A private offering does not have to be fully registered with the SEC.

prospectus   A registration statement required by the SEC before public companies and their underwriters can sell stocks or bonds to the public. The SEC passes on the completeness of the financial material presented, but such registration is not an endorsement by the government agency. Rather, the prospectus is meant to reveal all the material facts that might influence a potential investor. Preliminary drafts of the prospectus without the final offering price (circulated to generate interest in the financial community) have a printed red warning indicating that it has not yet received government approval; hence the colloquial reference to the booklet as a red herring, which recalls the days when such registration statements were misleading.

proxy   Every voting share in a public company can participate in the annual meeting, especially to vote on important business that comes before the shareholders. Of course, many shareowners are unable to attend, but they can nevertheless register their votes through proxy ballots or designate others to represent them.

put option   *See* **option.**

random selection and/or random walk   Whether it is a monkey throwing darts or the free flight of molecules, there is no discernible pattern to the activity under way. In the stock market, it is a theory that suggests no relation between transactions, no trends and no direction to security prices. Since all prices are independent, security analysis lacks predictive capability and is thus not particularly valuable.

registered bonds   Increasingly, registered bonds are the wave of tomorrow. The federal government now requires all municipal underwritings to issue registered bonds. Whether buying municipals or corporate issues, the purchaser is registered on the issuer's books and is automatically entitled to interest payments and redemption. On the other hand, bearer bonds still exist in the marketplace with their attached interest coupons, which must be presented to a paying agent to receive interest. Since anyone who possesses a bearer bond is the purported owner, there is obviously an element of risk in owning them. However, they do assure anonymity and secrecy.

repos   The short form for repurchase agreements between dealers in government and other fixed-interest securities and banks. Dealers need borrowed funds to carry their large inventories. They can "borrow" against their inventory as collateral—either overnight or for weeks—and then reverse the process. In reality, they first sell the securities with the understanding that they will purchase them back. Repos are a major tool for the Federal Reserve System in its day-to-day monetary management. If the Fed wants to ease money conditions, it enters the market, about noon each day, and lends dealers funds. The dealers use T-bills as collateral, and their checking accounts are credited, thus increasing bank reserves. At the end of the agreed time, the transaction is reversed as dealers buy back their T-bills. If the Fed wants to tighten, they buy first and sell later.

revenue bonds   Municipal bonds that generate their earnings from the fees or charges levied by the project they finance. A local port authority pays off its bondholders by the schedule of fees it charges those using its facility.

risk aversion   Risk-averse investors attempt to reduce risk on a given investment by diversifying, by buying calls or index options. The risk-averse investor is likely to have a lower rate of return on his funds since he may use a variety of hedges (all of which cost money) to reduce risk.

round lot   Common stocks are customarily traded in round lots of 100 shares. Anything less is considered an odd lot.

sell short/short sale   The sale of borrowed stock, usually provided by one's broker, with the hope that prices will decline so that the shares may be purchased and replaced at lower prices. The difference, after commissions and returning the dividends to the owners, is the profit from the short sale. The most a short seller can make is 100 percent on his money. But should the market move the wrong way, the potential for loss is infinite. So while it is almost as easy to sell short as buy long, less than 3 percent of investors work that side of the market.

short-term   An investment or asset held less than one year. Tax rates are unfavorable for short-term capital gains since they are treated as ordinary income. In addition, some investments (in commodities, short sales, etc.) are always considered as short-term no matter how long the holding or the open position.

specialist   A broker who specializes in one or just a few securities on the floor of an exchange. He presides over the auction and maintains a book of limit or stop orders. He is also charged with maintaining a fair and orderly market, which means that on occasion he must trade for his own account against the tide.

spot market   The spot market for commodities is one in which the immediate transaction is for a cash settlement.

stop order   A stop order can provide some protection on both the buy and sell sides. A stop order to sell, sometimes called a stop-loss order, is an instruction to the broker to sell your shares if a given price is touched during trading. In brief, it can be used to protect a profit by automatically selling out a position. On the other side, a stop order to buy is an instruction to buy shares if the price is touched, either on the way down or the way up.

street name   Securities left with a brokerage house are said to be in street name, meaning they are registered to the brokerage house, which then credits your account. The broker passes on dividends and informs you of any communications from the company. As a custodian of your property, a broker is strictly regulated by exchanges and federal agencies. In addition, a brokerage house has insurance to compensate its customers should it fail. Shares held in street name are probably every bit as secure as in your own safe deposit box—and far more convenient in the normal course of business.

tax anticipation bills and notes   These, and other anticipation notes, are usually very short term, for use until long-term financing can be arranged or until revenues come due. Occasionally the Treasury issues tax anticipation bills, which can be used by businesses to pay their income tax. Municipalities issue tax anticipation notes to finance their operating budgets until their tax receipts are in hand.

tender offer   In order to acquire or control another company, the acquiring company frequently makes a tender offer in cash for the shares of the company. Sometimes the offer is part cash and part common or preferred stock of the soliciting company. In either case, the tender offer is priced considerably above the trading price of the stock as an inducement for the shareholders to tender their shares. Some tender offers are friendly, usually an agreement or understanding by both boards of directors. But sometimes they are hostile or three-way fights that lead to a bidding up of the shares of the takeover candidate—generally to the advantage of stockholders.

TIGR (tiger)   A form of zero-coupon securities based on Treasury notes or bonds. Issued by an investment banking house, Treasury Investment Growth Receipts pay no interest until maturity. Their advantage is that they lock in a yield for the duration of the underlying issue with no need to be concerned over what to do with semiannual interest of interest-paying bonds. Some investment bankers call them cats (Certificates of Account on Treasury Securities).

tombstone   An advertisement in the financial press, bordered with funereal black, listing the names of the underwriters for a particular issue along with the significant offering terms. Frequently the issue has been completely sold out before the tombstone appears and the notice is only a matter of record.

underwriter   *See* **investment banker.**

uptick   For a short sale, the transaction must be made in a rising market or on an uptick—at least ⅛ of a point higher than the previous transaction. However, a short sale can be completed even on a zero uptick if the penultimate sale was higher than the previous one. Some technicians measure the internal strength of the market by devising a ratio of all uptick sales against downtick sales.

wash sale   A wash sale is the buying and selling of the same security, an act that generates volume but not necessarily a change in price. Wash sales in volume were an abuse of markets in the 1920s and were subsequently restricted by the SEC. For tax purposes, a wash sale is buying and selling the same security within a 30-day period. A capital loss is denied if the same security or an option on the same security is repurchased within 30 days. However, there is some debate on whether calls of different expiration dates or striking prices are indeed identical securities. In the bond market, tax switching or swaps at the end of the year can establish capital losses, but the repurchase of other bonds of different issuers with the same yield, rating and maturity would not constitute a wash sale.

yield curve   The relationship of yield to years of maturity. The yield curve is a reflection—perhaps "distillation" is more to the point—of all known information of business conditions and interest rate prospects. A normal yield curve (a continuous curve sloping upward to the right) suggests that in the short end, yields are lower, but as the maturities lengthen, the yields must rise to compensate lenders for greater uncertainty of future events. In periods of political turbulence, economic uncertainty and near-runaway inflation, the yield curve changes dramatically. Lenders will demand extraordinarily high short-term rates, but perhaps somewhat less interest in the intermediate period, if they are willing to lend at all. Such conditions will show a yield curve that is almost inverted.

zero-coupon bonds   Bonds issued without provisions for semiannual interest. They are sold at a discount so that the annual accrued interest is paid at maturity. There are a number of variations to this relatively new type of bond, the value of which has much to do with one's tax status.

INDEX